When a Loved One Has
Borderline Personality Disorder

WHEN A LOVED ONE HAS BORDERLINE PERSONALITY DISORDER

A Compassionate Guide to Building a Healthy and Supportive Relationship

Daniel S. Lobel, PhD

ROCKRIDGE
PRESS

For general information on our other products and services or to obtain technical support, please contact our Customer Care Department within the United States at (866) 744-2665, or outside the United States at (510) 253-0500.

Rockridge Press publishes its books in a variety of electronic and print formats. Some content that appears in print may not be available in electronic books, and vice versa.

Interior and Cover Designer: John Calmeyer
Art Producer: Megan Baggott
Editor: Katherine De Chant
Production Editor: Caroline Flanagan
Production Manager: Holly Haydash

Paperback ISBN: 978-1-63878-490-6
eBook ISBN: 978-1-63878-665-8
R0

I would like to dedicate this book to those who have the devotion to work on a relationship with a loved one with BPD symptoms and the strength to walk away if necessary. For many people, it is easiest to just walk away from a difficult relationship. This avoids taking responsibility for aspects of what went wrong and eliminates the need to work on the self for the benefit of the relationship.

If you love someone and they suffer from a disorder that affects their relationship with you, then you face a challenge. When your loved one has BPD, you will work hard and you may get hurt. If you are successful, you will be rewarded with a healthier relationship.

If you are not successful, you will know that you tried your best. This book is also dedicated to those who have the strength to walk away from a relationship rather than enabling it.

No matter your situation, you deserve a healthy relationship with a partner who is capable of participating.

CONTENTS

INTRODUCTION

My professional focus on personality disorders in general, and borderline personality disorder (BPD) in particular, was strongly influenced by my experience as a court-appointed neutral child-custody forensic examiner. I was assigned to cases by the supreme and family courts where one or both parents' custody was challenged due to potential negligence or abuse. A large part of my job involved talking to children who were hurt by their parents or hurt because their parents did not protect them sufficiently.

Physical and sexual abuse, once identified, were dealt with by child protective services. It was much more difficult to get the legal system to address emotional mistreatment. In most cases, the emotional mistreatment was caused by parents who suffered from personality disorders or other mental illnesses that impact their behaviors toward their children and other people they are close to.

Some of these parents caused significant pain and harm to their children because of their illness. But it was also clear that they loved their children and were fighting to stay connected to them. The children, in most of these cases, loved their parents even though they often were frightened of them and had been hurt by them. You might recognize this dynamic in your own relationship with someone who has diagnosed BPD, whether it's a parent, spouse, sibling, or friend.

If you have a loved one with symptoms of BPD, then you know how difficult it is to reconcile strong emotions that conflict with one another. You feel their love, but not all the time. You feel their rage, but not all the time. You may wonder how they can hurt someone they love. You probably question your reasons for being in a relationship where you often get hurt, or wonder if the good outweighs the bad.

Loving someone with symptoms of BPD can be complex and overwhelming. It is strongly recommended that you seek support, whether it's in the form of professional services, helpful organizations, or support groups. At the end of this book, you will find a list of resources (page 147) that are available to people who are going through what you are dealing with. You don't have to go it alone.

Your relationship can have negative effects on your own mental health if you do not address the hurtful behaviors that are driven by BPD. If you already have symptoms such as significant anxiety, depression, headaches, or high blood pressure, you need to seek out appropriate medical treatment for these maladies. This book will increase your awareness of your situation and provide tools to help you cope, but it is not a substitute for professional consultation.

HOW TO USE THIS BOOK

The first three chapters of this book will take you through an understanding of what BPD is, how it affects your loved one, how it affects your relationship, and how it affects you personally. Many people who have loved ones with symptoms of BPD know that there is something wrong, but they don't understand what it is. The first half of this book offers some clarity.

The second half of the book focuses on what you can do and what could happen if you do nothing. Once you understand the situation, you will have to make some difficult decisions about how to proceed in this relationship. Each chapter offers a "mindful minute" exercise to help you reflect on what is happening to you. The focus of this reflection is to take care of yourself as you endeavor to either change or end a struggling relationship. You cannot be in a healthy relationship unless you are healthy and taking care of yourself.

Keeping a journal throughout the process you are about to embark on is strongly suggested. Numerous suggestions are offered throughout the book as to how you might journal events, thoughts, behaviors, and feelings, but you should use whatever format is most effective for you.

An Important Safety Reminder

Many individuals with symptoms of BPD engage in self-harming behaviors, including suicide attempts. These behaviors should always be taken very seriously. In chapter 7, you will learn specific techniques for recognizing and managing these situations.

One of the resources offered at the end of this book (page 147) is the National Suicide Prevention Lifeline, a U.S.-based suicide prevention network of over 160 crisis centers that provide 24/7 service via a toll-free hotline at 1-800-273-8255. It is available to anyone in suicidal crisis or emotional distress.

The Importance of Protecting Yourself

Individuals with symptoms of BPD are more likely to physically harm themselves than others, though it is very common for them to lash out at those they are close to. This can sometimes get physical, but is most often emotional. It is very important going forward that you do not allow your loved one to hurt you. This is dangerous to you, and it makes them sicker. Chapters 6 and 7 offer tools for dealing with lashing-out behavior while keeping yourself safe and well. In urgent situations, you can also contact the National Domestic Violence Hotline at 1-800-799-7233.

1 Understanding BPD

Personality disorder is one of the most difficult forms of mental illness to understand and diagnose. In this chapter, you will understand what makes borderline personality disorder (BPD) distinct from other psychiatric disorders. One of the difficulties of diagnosing this disorder is that, unlike people with most other mental disorders, individuals with BPD do not recognize their symptoms as symptoms, and so they do not acknowledge or report them. Most individuals with BPD actually have to be convinced that there is anything wrong with them at all. This is because part of the disease is a tendency to blame others for the problems in their lives, so they don't recognize that there is anything wrong with them. As you read through the descriptions of the symptoms presented in this chapter, keep in mind that you are seeing aspects of your loved one that they might not recognize in themself. This will dictate how you can discuss the effects of their symptoms on you, which we will discuss in the next chapter. •

What Is BPD?

The term *borderline personality disorder* was first described by Adolf Stern (Stern, 1938) as a disorder that has aspects of both neurosis (anxiety) and psychosis (thought disorder). It is on the border between the two.

The current definition, according to the American Psychiatric Association's *Diagnostic and Statistical Manual, 5th Edition* (APA, 2013), is "a pervasive pattern of instability of interpersonal relationships, self-image, and affects and marked impulsivity, beginning by early adulthood and present in a variety of contexts." The nine symptoms that describe this instability are listed in the next section. The disorder is considered to be present when five or more of these symptoms are present.

The symptoms must be present in a *pervasive pattern* and in *a variety of contexts*, meaning they must occur in different relationships and places—with colleagues in the workplace, home with family, etc.

The combination of symptoms causes instability in many areas of functioning, the clearest indication being the instability caused in the relationship you have with the loved one with BPD. The person can go from hot to cold very quickly, seemingly without reason or warning. You may notice instability in their self-image as they seem entitled in many circumstances and yet have periods of self-loathing during which they hurt themself. Impulsivity is a form of unstable behavior, driven substantially or completely by emotion without the sound judgment that logical thought offers.

The various combinations of the following nine symptoms result in different patterns of behavior in different individuals. In addition, it is very common for individuals with BPD to have other illnesses, or comorbidities, at the same time such as anxiety disorders, mood disorders, eating disorders, and substance abuse disorders.

9 SYMPTOMS OF BPD

Frantic effort to avoid real or imagined abandonment
BPD causes sufferers to experience high levels of anxiety when they feel abandoned or think that they might be abandoned. The anxiety levels can be so high as to cause panic attacks or other panic-level anxiety symptoms.

If your loved one is with you, you will notice clingy behaviors. They will attempt to discourage you from leaving them. This can also occur during phone calls or video chats. If your loved one is not with you, they will compel you to call them or be with them.

If you don't respond as quickly as they expect you to, they may become frantic. They may claim to have an emergency or threaten to hurt themself if you don't get back to them right away. They may lash out at you and accuse you of not caring about them. They may experience a panic attack. You will probably find this exhausting.

A pattern of intense interpersonal relationships characterized by alternating extremes of idealization and devaluation
Individuals with BPD tend to think in binary, black-and-white, terms. They tend to love things or hate things. They describe things in extreme terms as being excellent or horrible. They view you in the same terms.

One of the first things you will notice is that they tend to bond very quickly. When they first meet you, they will quickly treat you as a close friend, sharing their intimate thoughts and feelings. They will probably contact you frequently, and they may tell you that they love you early on in the relationship.

They expect you to be more empathic and thoughtful toward them than anyone else, including yourself. They idealize you early in the relationship, which turns to devaluing you later because they have expectations of you that you cannot sustain, so you will inevitably disappoint them. When that happens, they may lash out at you or ghost you (not respond to your efforts to contact them). Their binary view of things is not stable. They may alternate between loving and hating you, and a relationship with them may feel like a roller coaster.

Identity disturbance: markedly and persistently unstable self-image or sense of self

BPD sufferers see themselves in idealized and devalued terms, similar to the way they see others. They frequently switch between states of self-loathing, when they disappoint themselves or they feel slighted by others, and self-adoration, when they feel successful or validated by others.

When they have a positive self-image, they engage in pleasurable and healthy activities. They eat a good meal, make an appointment to have their teeth cleaned, socialize with friends, etc. They are less needy during these times and more tolerant.

When they have a negative self-image, they experience self-loathing and become less focused on taking care of themselves. This is when they get needy and reach out, sometimes frantically. If they don't get a suitable response, they may express their self-loathing in self-destructive ways, such as by cutting or burning themselves.

What you will notice is that individuals with BPD put a strong emphasis on validation from others to feel good about themselves. If you fail to validate them, or if they perceive you as slighting them, such as by not inviting them to a party or not returning their call quickly enough, they get hurt. This increases their self-loathing and their likelihood of lashing out.

—

Impulsivity in at least two areas that are potentially self-damaging (e.g., spending, sex, substance abuse, binge eating)

Impulsive behaviors are unpredictable and driven by emotion, rather than reasoning. BPD causes sufferers to experience their emotions very intensely. This is called *dysregulation*. Because the emotions are very intense, it is more difficult for the person to apply coping mechanisms, which results in impulsivity.

The form of impulsivity most disruptive to relationships is the unfiltered expression of anger, aggression, or frustration. Often referred to as lashing out, BPD dysregulation causes sufferers to say hurtful things to loved ones when they are frustrated or feel slighted. This most often takes the form of verbal criticism or accusation, but can also manifest in breaking things, throwing things, punching walls, etc.

Other forms of impulsivity tend to be either overtly self-destructive, such as cutting or head banging, or significantly increase the risk of self-harm, such as driving too fast or driving intoxicated, confronting dangerous individuals, or breaking laws that are considered inconvenient, such as curfews, driving on closed roads, or shoplifting.

Other impulsive behaviors are driven by pleasure-seeking emotions, such as spending beyond one's means, unhealthy consumption of alcohol, drugs, or food, and unsafe sexual behaviors. Because these behaviors are not driven by logic or thought, they are not able to be corrected through reasoning.

Recurrent suicidal behavior, gestures, or threats, or self-mutilating behavior

In sufferers of BPD, threatening to hurt or kill themselves may be used to manipulate people. When feeling neglected or abandoned, BPD sufferers frequently make statements such as "I might as well just kill myself. You probably wouldn't even notice." It is not unusual for sufferers to engage in self-destructive behaviors in front of others to try to manipulate them. This might include cutting or burning themselves, or taking a handful of pills or ingesting toxic substances.

Individuals who suffer from BPD also often mutilate themselves in private. Cutting or burning of the skin is a very common expression of self-loathing. BPD sufferers generally describe that feeling physical pain gives them relief from emotional pain; however, what brings some temporary relief in the short term makes things worse in the long run by producing a physical wound, which is an enduring reminder to them of their self-loathing.

Another function of suicidal threats or self-harming behavior is to avoid unwanted or threatening activities, such as school, work, or uncomfortable social situations. The self-harming behaviors are often presented as accidents, such as a fall or an accident with a kitchen knife.

Most of these suicidal and self-mutilative threats and gestures are not meant to be fatal; however, these behaviors should be treated as potentially very dangerous.

Affective instability due to a marked reactivity of mood

Individuals with BPD are often described as very emotional. BPD causes dysregulation of their emotions or affects. It accentuates their experience of emotions to such a degree that they cannot use their intelligence to understand or modulate them, and so they blurt out their emotions often before they understand them. The emotions are expressed, unfiltered, in real time, as they occur.

The result of this is that their emotions and mood are unstable. They fluctuate quickly in reaction to whatever is occurring at the moment. They feel well when they like the way things are going, but the moment something does not go their way, they become frustrated or angry and may lash out.

These emotions and moods tend to be very intense, but remarkably transient. They can recover from frustration or anger very quickly once the cause of these emotions is dealt with. Loved ones are often baffled by how BPD sufferers can be lashing out at one moment and then friendly moments later.

Chronic feelings of emptiness

Individuals with BPD often feel like part of themselves is missing. Healthy adults have a stable core sense of self that gives them a secure base—they know who they are. They don't change their sense of self just because something displeases them. They don't need excessive praise from others in order to feel worthy. But individuals with BPD lack a stable core sense of self and so they seek to fill the gap with validation from the people around them. For this reason, individuals with BPD are extremely sensitive to criticism.

These chronic feelings of emptiness often create a sense of need so intense that the sufferer is rarely satisfied with what they get from others in terms of responsiveness or admiration. They are frequently disappointed with others, and they express this in real time. This causes instability in relationships as it makes those who love them feel inadequate and unappreciated.

Inappropriate, intense anger or difficulty controlling anger

BPD sufferers often have angry outbursts both in public and private settings. While it is normal for humans to get angry when they are hurt, people with BPD take it to a whole new level. They don't keep their pain a secret, but rather wear it with a sort of pride (which may come across as self-pity) to reinforce both their need to be taken care of and their victim status. They often lash out at those they perceive to be responsible for the hurt they are experiencing.

Their outbursts might take the form of verbal and/or physical attacks, breaking objects, or using objects as weapons. The anger may also be expressed passively, such as by speaking poorly of someone or undermining their efforts to succeed at something important to them.

Due to the affective emotional dysregulation that BPD causes, these angry responses are disproportional to whatever it is they are responding to. The BPD causes them to experience an intensified form of frustration and anger and their expression is intensified as well. This causes very significant instability in relationships as it pushes away those they are trying to be close to.

Transient, stress-related paranoid ideation or severe dissociative symptoms

Both paranoid ideation and dissociation are types of instability of thought and perception, during which an affected person sees things differently.

Paranoid ideation is when an individual experiences unrealistic concerns that others are working against them or trying to hurt them. These feelings accompany periods of negative self-image and the associated self-loathing. In order to lessen feelings of self-loathing, they blame others for difficulties in their lives rather than taking responsibility, seeing themself as the victim. When their mood and self-perception improve, they experience less paranoid ideation.

Experienced by many individuals with BPD, dissociation takes the form of feeling like things are not real, that they themselves are not real, or that they are experiencing their lives as observers rather than participants. Mild to moderate dissociation is akin to "spacing out"—being internally focused and unresponsive to one's environment for a short period of time. Severe forms of dissociation can involve fugue states, which involve losing hours or even days where they do not know what happened to them.

Dissociation generally occurs in reaction to anxiety or stress, such as a perceived threat. The greater the perception of the threat, the more profound the symptoms of dissociation. When the threat is absent, the dissociative state generally resolves fairly quickly.

WRITE IT DOWN

Now that you have a framework for understanding the symptoms of BPD, you can organize your thoughts about how it affects your relationship with a loved one with BPD. It will be helpful for you to use a journal to categorize the different aspects of your relationship.

A useful exercise at this point is to consider the patterns of behavior that trouble you not only in the context of BPD, but also in the context of healthy functioning. Many if not all of the symptoms on pages 3–9 can be found in mild forms in individuals who do not have a personality disorder. Not all annoying aspects of intimate relationships are pathological.

What Causes BPD?

Three factors are generally considered to be the causes of BPD. Each cause influences the development of BPD in a different way and the more of these factors that are present, the more likely a person is to have BPD.

GENETICS

Indirect evidence supports the belief that BPD is the result of a genetic deviation. The American Psychological Association (APA) reports that BPD is five times more common among first-degree relatives of sufferers than the general population. A recent study showed that BPD has some genetic overlap with bipolar disorder, major depression, and schizophrenia; however, studies to date have failed to identify a specific gene mutation responsible for BPD. Further research is ongoing that seeks to map a BPD gene.

BIOLOGY

An extensive review of neuroimaging studies found several differences, regarding both anatomical structure and neurochemical dynamics, in the way the brains of individuals with BPD function as compared to non-sufferers (Lis et al., 2007). It is not yet clear whether these differences are caused by different genetic makeup, or are a result of experiences that cause BPD symptoms that also cause variation in brain function.

ENVIRONMENTAL FACTORS

It is generally thought that environmental factors interact with genetic and biological factors in the development of BPD symptoms. A recent review of studies has found that individuals with BPD are more likely to have been victims of childhood maltreatment than non-affected individuals (Ibrahim, 2018). This review also found that mistreated children are more likely to develop BPD symptoms than children who were not mistreated.

In my clinical practice, I find that individuals who develop BPD tend to be raised by parents who have difficulty disciplining and setting boundaries. These parents give in to their child's protests and rants, thus rewarding this behavior. This we will refer to as *feeding the illness*. The BPD gets fed when others give in to angry outbursts or other hurtful efforts at manipulation. This is the biggest error that those trying to be in a relationship with a BPD sufferer can make: giving in to, and thus enabling, hurtful behaviors. More on this will be discussed in chapter 5.

Many individuals with BPD report a history of child abuse or other childhood trauma. The American Psychiatric Association reports that "Physical and sexual abuse, neglect, hostile conflict and early parental loss are more common in the childhood histories of those with borderline personality disorder" (APA, 2013). Many of these individuals have active or residual posttraumatic stress disorder (PTSD).

The interaction between these two disorders, BPD and PTSD, is very complex. BPD causes sufferers to experience emotions in an intensified form, which is also true for PTSD symptoms. This can make it very difficult to tell whether one is experiencing a painful or frightening flashback of a traumatic experience of childhood, or whether they are being dramatic in an effort to get validation or avoid abandonment. You will find resources for understanding PTSD and how to be supportive while dealing with other symptoms of BPD in the Resources section of this book (page 147).

BPD Isn't Monolithic

You will notice that I often refer to individuals with symptoms of BPD, rather than focusing on the diagnosis itself. This is to remind us that each of the nine symptoms of BPD appear in other disorders and many of them, to some degree, also appear in emotionally healthy individuals. BPD is defined as a cluster of symptoms—any five out of the nine criteria. It has many different forms, and some of the symptoms are absent in many who experience this disorder. BPD is further diversified by the many comorbid illnesses that interact with the symptoms of BPD.

The most prominent feature of this disorder is instability, and the symptoms themselves may be unstable in an individual. Some of them may become dormant for years, while others emerge depending on the person's circumstances. For example, it is common for individuals who self-mutilate to stop this behavior for a period of time. Sometimes the symptom can be replaced by a different symptom, such as other impulsive behaviors.

Even with all of this diversity of symptoms, some patterns of behavior and relating are so fundamental to the disorder that they appear consistently. These are the ones that this book focuses on.

How BPD Affects Relationships

Each symptom of BPD has a different effect on relationships with loved ones, and they all interact. Everyone has a different experience loving and living with a person with symptoms of BPD.

The most striking effect of BPD on relationships is instability, which has a devastating effect on trust. The ability to trust another individual requires reliability, dependability, loyalty, and, most important, stability. Because of the frequent changes in affect and mood, it is very hard to feel secure in relationships with individuals who suffer from BPD symptoms.

Trying to be close to a person you do not trust causes anxiety. Over time, many people who have loved ones that suffer from symptoms of BPD become increasingly anxious about interacting with their loved one. The uncertainty of whether you will find a friendly, loving, and welcoming loved one or whether you will find a disappointed, dissatisfied loved one who is critical and rejecting creates anxiety.

You may find yourself feeling tested. Because of their persistent need for reassurance from others, every act or instance of inaction is looked at by them as a measure of whether you love them or care about them enough, since they judge you based on their neediness and emptiness, rather than any objective criteria.

This continually stresses the relationship. For many loved ones, it leads them to avoidance, especially after they have been pushed back by criticism or lashing out, and this becomes a self-fulfilling prophecy for the BPD-symptom sufferer. They push you away and then blame you for not being a good partner, friend, or relative. Then you avoid more. Then they push harder.

If you are not avoidant, then you might confront your loved one for pushing you away and then blaming you because they feel empty and alone. In most situations, this will not be fruitful. They will only blame you more. In the coming chapters, you will learn skills developed specifically for those who love individuals suffering from BPD symptoms.

Living with BPD

When dealing with loved ones with symptoms of BPD, it is important that you not equate them with their condition. You don't blame people who are sick for being sick. It's important to strive for compassion toward people who suffer from BPD, especially when you love them. Refocus frustration and anger on the disease, and not the individual. The disease is a monster, and you need to join your loved one in fighting the disease.

In order to do this, you will need to have boundaries. Boundaries are tools to prevent your loved one's disease from compelling them to hurt you. You cannot help your loved one while they are hurting you, so you must protect yourself by setting boundaries.

TREATMENT CAN MAKE A DIFFERENCE

There are many treatments available for individuals suffering from symptoms of BPD as well as those who love them. These treatments are effective and should be used as much as possible to support you, your loved one, and your relationship with that individual. In chapter 4, you'll learn more about specific treatment options available for BPD and the significant impact they can have.

You must always keep in mind that in order to have a healthy relationship, you must be healthy and practice healthy habits. Allowing people you love to hurt you is not healthy. In chapters 5 and 6, you will learn how to protect yourself and practice self-care while you seek to have the best relationship you can with your loved one despite the fact that they suffer from symptoms of BPD.

For many of you, this chapter was a real eye-opener. If you are like most loved ones, you have been feeling some tension or the sense that things were uncomfortable or not right, but you probably just couldn't put your finger on it. Now that you understand some of the patterns of this disorder, you are probably recalling and recognizing instances of some of the behavior patterns in your transactions with your loved one. You may be feeling overwhelmed.

Times when you feel overwhelmed, anxious, or attacked are times when self-care is imperative. We nurture ourselves. We heal ourselves. Never beat yourself up.

When feeling strong feelings, or waves of strong emotion or anxiety, the first thing to do is not to react. Take a moment to absorb it all. Our initial feelings about significant events are often different from what we feel once we have time to inquire and process events that have just occurred.

Develop for yourself a set of activities that reliably make you feel relaxed, pampered, and well. This may be a bath, a nap, a workout, playing an instrument, etc. Engage in one of these activities while you reflect on your understanding of events and your feelings about them.

Once you have restored calmness, you should journal your reaction to the event and how you coped with it. This will help consolidate your increasing tool kit of coping strategies.

Key Takeaways

- BPD is a complex and diverse disorder. This makes it hard to identify and understand.

- BPD is often further complicated by comorbid disorders.

- Emotional dysregulation causes sufferers of BPD symptoms to experience their emotions more intensively than non-sufferers.

- The different symptoms of BPD have different effects on relationships with loved ones.

- There are patterns to the instability that can be identified and used to strategize a better relationship with your loved one.

2 What BPD Might Look Like in Your Relationship

Borderline personality disorder affects entire families in many different ways. Individuals with symptoms of BPD often exhibit patterns of behaviors with those they are close with that cause others pain and create dysfunction in the relationship. Many individuals whose loved ones have BPD are confused and frustrated by how often the relationship causes conflict and pain. Many of these people end up blaming themselves. In this chapter, you will learn how to identify these relationship patterns. In later chapters, you will learn how these patterns affect you and what you can do to protect yourself and improve your relationship. ●

Can You Relate?

In this chapter, you'll find dialogues and vignettes that illustrate patterns of relating that are characteristic of this disorder, and tools and techniques you can use to protect yourself and improve the relationship with your loved one affected by BPD. These dialogues are based on real cases from my 30 years of clinical practice. The names of the individuals, as well as many of the facts, have been changed to protect their privacy.

Following are the stories of four different individuals as they struggled to figure out what was happening in their relationships. They all share common characteristics, the most significant being that all of these individuals are in a great deal of pain and distress resulting from patterns of behavior in relationships with individuals they love.

If you recognize yourself in these situations, your loved one might be suffering symptoms of BPD. In the previous chapter, you learned what the symptoms of BPD look like and how they affect the ways in which your loved one relates to you. Now you'll see some of the symptoms in practice.

AMY'S JOURNEY: HOW CAN A MOTHER WHO TRIES SO HARD BE SO AWFUL?

My heart is completely broken. I have devoted my life to this child and she hates me. Everything I do is wrong in her eyes. She tells me that I ruined her life. How did I do this? I would change. I would do anything. I am afraid that once she finishes college, she will have nothing to do with me.

Her father left us for another woman when Julie was three. She had been difficult as a baby. She always pushed me away when I tried to hold her or comfort her. When she was upset, she was inconsolable. She had a very hard time accepting no for an answer and was very impatient. She made me feel guilty, like I was a bad parent.

The situation got worse when Brian left. There was no warning. We just woke up one day and he was gone. I devoted myself to Julie. I felt that I owed it to her, especially now that she had to grow up without a father. She got more irritable. I felt more guilty. By the time she was a teenager, I gave in to her every time. I thought if I could just please her enough, she would be happy with the childhood that I had to offer her. Now she is away at school. She only calls when she needs something.

I get along with everyone else quite well. I am successful at work, appreciated, and well-liked. Why can't my daughter treat me this way? My friends think maybe it's her and I am starting to believe them. She will never let me feel like I have been a good mother, no matter what I do.

BRENDA FINDS IT'S NOT IN THE BOTTLE

It's like living with two different men. When Jeff is good, he can be really good. He is a great provider and we have been able to travel and enjoy some leisure time.

When he is bad, he really scares me. He starts with accusatory statements like "I understand now why you don't love me. I am not exciting enough for you," and "I see you have lost some weight. I wish I was the guy you were doing it for." Then he goes into full-blown accusations of my only loving him for his money or of having affairs with various friends and neighbors. It seemed to be related to his use of alcohol. The more he drank, the nastier he got. We lost some friends because of his accusations.

After bad days, he would approach me lovingly as though nothing had happened. He blamed my not being affectionate to him on my not loving him or loving someone else. He could not seem to accept that my lack of affection was because of his behavior.

Then he crossed the line. He started to get physical with me when he was in his nasty mood. He tried to slap me, and I left our home. I told him that he had to stop drinking if he wanted me to come home. So he stopped drinking.

At first, things were better. There was some tension between us, but he was definitely in better control. I started to get more comfortable and behaved affectionately toward him. He seemed to like this. Until one day, I had a conversation with my father on the phone.

After the call, Jeff asked who I was talking to. He didn't believe that I was talking to my father. This turned into a very bad situation, and I thought he was going to try to hit me again. I thought he must have slipped with his sobriety. I could not find any evidence, and he insisted that he had not had alcohol since he stopped drinking.

I believed him. The alcohol makes his condition worse, but even without the alcohol he is unstable. I also came to realize that it was not me. He frequently claimed that my behavior was unloving and suggestive of someone having an affair. I knew that I was not cheating on him but I desperately tried to change my behavior so that he would stop accusing me. Now I understand why that would never work.

CARLOS: I WAS ABUSED. HOW DID I MISS IT?

As soon as I agree to see my mother, I start to get tense. I can't seem to think about anything else. I have difficulty focusing on work. Then comes the nightmare. The details are different but the theme is the same. I am in some familiar and comfortable place, feeling peaceful and safe. Then the monsters come. I get up and run or swim, and they come after me. I awake frightened. Then the migraines start.

I basically suffer until the day comes to see her. I have to plan how to respond to nonstop subtle and not-so-subtle attacks. When I was a kid, she would beat me if I didn't do what she wanted. Her rage was frightening. I always was afraid that she would lose control and kill me.

Now that I'm older, she still gets that look, and her eyes fill with rage. Her face gets tight. I lose my breath. She then asks questions until she can find something I say to criticize and then she humiliates me for my choices or beliefs. I often feel I would rather get hit then deal with this slow freeze-out.

Most of my life, I felt guilty for not wanting to see her more. Now I ask myself, why do I see her when it causes me such suffering? And why am I suffering so extremely? I went to see the counselor at work and she suggested that I might have some post-traumatic stress disorder. I told her that I was not in the military. She clarified that she was referring to my being a victim of child abuse. Suddenly, things that were confusing for so long started to make sense to me. I am forty-five years old, and now is the first time that it even occurred to me that I had something to protect myself from. Forty-five years of child abuse. How did I miss it?

FRIENDS WITH TOO MANY BENEFITS? SHERRY'S DILEMMA

Robbi and I were friends since high school. We drifted apart as we built lives with other people, but then I became single. Later, Robbi and I shared an apartment. We called ourselves the odd couple. It was really nice to not have to come home to an empty apartment at night.

Living with Robbi brought out a side of her that I had not seen before. She didn't seem to have any regard for my belongings or my space. She would eat my food and not replace it. She would come into my bedroom without knocking. She often did not clean up after herself.

When I tried to speak to her about it, she was defensive. She said that I was making her feel unwelcome. She called me a narcissist and accused me of being controlling and obsessive. I am not sure why, but I apologized to her. Maybe I was feeling guilty that I had made her feel unwelcome.

She started to cry and hugged me. Then she kissed me. I had never kissed a woman before, but I let it happen. We had a very nice evening, but we agreed that we were not in love. Just friends with benefits.

This made our other issues worse. Robbi felt more entitled to my belongings. She started to borrow my clothing without asking and then return it uncleaned. She sometimes climbed into my bed while I was sleeping.

I tried to confront her on some of these behaviors and she got even more defensive. Anytime I asked her to change her behavior in any way, she attacked me. She accused me of all kinds of things and screamed at me in a tone that was frightening and threatening.

Can I get out of this situation without losing Robbi as a friend? Do I still want to be her friend? Is this my fault? Did I set this up?

WRITE IT DOWN

As you read on and embark on your journey of personal growth, I strongly suggest that you create a journal, if you don't already have one. You will find this useful in many ways, such as:

- Writing thoughts and feelings down causes your brain to process them at a deeper level.

- Growth is built on prior growth. As you begin to see and feel things differently, you will want to look back on the beginnings of your journey as a reference point.

- If you decide to confront your loved one, it will help to have some examples of situations that made you feel hurt or uncomfortable. We will discuss later how best to present this information.

The format of your journal is flexible, but I suggest that it be chronological in the order in which events occur. Some people find it useful to keep a narrative format, like telling a story or a diary, while others prefer to keep bullet points of thoughts, feelings, and events. You should choose whatever format works best for you.

Here is a list of common signs of the effects of BPD on relationships. Patterns of behavior are significant if they occur frequently or persistently. Check off the following behavior patterns only if they are repeated. The more items you check off, the more likely that BPD traits or tendencies are affecting your relationship.

This is not a diagnostic tool and should not be used to diagnose anyone with BPD. While these behaviors are reflective of BPD patterns, they are not unique to BPD. They could indicate other personality disorder traits or appear in the absence of any disorder.

- Your loved one does not take responsibility for themself. They may be very defensive when you try to point out to them mistakes they have made or ways that they have hurt you.

- You are often blamed for things that are not your fault.

- Your loved one is generally impatient with you and others. While they may be frequently late when you are waiting for them, they are clear that they do not like waiting for you.

- You often feel like you are not good enough in their eyes.

- You are accused of being disloyal when you pay attention to other people.

- You are accused of betraying them if you don't agree with them on everything.

- You are left holding the bag: paying for things, hosting, driving, etc.

- You are frequently tested: demands made that you would do if "you really cared."

- They hold you responsible for them not hurting themself. For example, they may say that they don't trust themself to not hurt themself and then demand that you be with them at a time that is not convenient to you.*

- They often have cuts, burns, or other abrasions that are not well explained.*

- You are held to ideals that are impossible for you to achieve and then accused of disappointing them.

If you checked off this item and your loved one is a minor, then you need to take protective action. If they are your child, you should seek professional help. If they are not your child, and you believe the child to be at risk, you should alert the parent and/or authorities to the situation.

Some of these behavior patterns are more troublesome than others, but in general, the presence of three or more of the behavior patterns on pages 26–27 suggests that BPD is interfering with your relationship.

What Does It All Mean?

The presence of behavior patterns that resemble BPD does not mean that your loved one has the disorder. This is one of the most difficult disorders to diagnose, and it has specific criteria that require observation of the person under many different circumstances. This book takes a pragmatic approach to this disorder, which involves focusing on behavior patterns rather than diagnoses.

The prognosis is largely determined by a single factor. If the individual is willing to join you, and perhaps mental health providers, against the illness, there is a good opportunity to have the individual heal and grow while the relationship heals and grows.

Bonding occurs and deepens as you and your loved one pursue a common goal to defeat this burdensome disease. The challenge is that the person affected by the BPD symptoms must acknowledge that their BPD-affected behaviors are disruptive to relationships and be willing to do something about it.

In practice, this means they have to acknowledge that the BPD symptoms cause them intense discomfort, which they express to their loved ones in hurtful ways. Once they can accept that they express their painful feelings as attacks on others, then they can work with you on expressing these feelings to you in ways that are not hurtful. Recognizing BPD as the common enemy, not your loved one, will benefit the relationship by increasing closeness.

If your loved one does not accept that they are hurting you in the process of expressing their feelings, then you will have to take measures that decrease closeness. If someone is hurting you, you must protect yourself by setting boundaries. For example, if your loved one puts you down or embarrasses you in front of your friends and refuses to stop, then you have to keep your loved one away from your friends. This will make you less close to your loved one.

You will probably be blamed for withdrawing and accused of being hurtful. It is important that you recognize that the reason you had to withdraw was because your loved one was hurting you, not because you are mean or don't love them.

While boundaries are healthy in relationships, if you have to erect one and then struggle to maintain or reinforce it, this does not bode well for the future of the relationship. This is because it does not allow for the cooperative process that can occur if your loved one accepts that they must fight the illness instead of fighting you.

What Should I Do Next?

The first step is to be clear with yourself about your boundaries and limits. You have to ask yourself the basic question of whether or not you will allow others to mistreat you. What are the limits of this mistreatment? Will you let others physically hurt you? How about emotional abuse? Will you allow others to make you feel bad about yourself? The answers to these questions will determine how you proceed with all relationships in your life.

Healthy individuals are not hurtful to the ones they love. When they do hurt those they love, they are contrite; they apologize and make amends where possible. It is very hard to feel loved by someone who has a pattern of hurting you.

Individuals with symptoms of BPD want to love and be loved. Unfortunately, BPD symptoms interfere with sufferers' ability to sustain a loving relationship. This is because BPD often causes sufferers to be hurtful to those they are close to when they are frustrated. This results in unstable and impaired attachments that are rarely if ever fully satisfying. This book is written for the non-affected loved ones of those who suffer from this disorder. Help is available to those who suffer from BPD, but is beyond the scope of this book. This book will show you how to support your loved one with BPD to seek treatment, but first we need to focus on your self-protection, healing, and growth.

The following chapters will help you define your limits and boundaries and show you how to protect yourself and set and maintain boundaries while you try to support your loved one in healing and growth.

· · · · · · · · · · · · · · · ·

TALK ABOUT IT

Talking about BPD with sufferers of BPD is tricky business. Many individuals ask me how to tell their loved ones that they might have BPD, in the hope that there will be an "aha" moment. In my experience, it usually does not go this way. Rather, they become offended, and the whole concept becomes painful and toxic, making it more difficult for them to heal.

What is more effective is focusing on the behavior patterns that we identified in this chapter and that you have logged in your journal. The first thing you should consider in talking to your loved one about BPD symptoms is timing. Bringing it up in the middle of an argument or conflict is the worst time. Because individuals with BPD experience emotional dysregulation, or instability, once they are upset, they only get more upset when you point out that something displeases you about them. This topic is best brought up during times of tranquility.

The best way to bring up BPD behaviors is to acknowledge the person's motives while pointing out that their method is unlikely to yield success. Here is an example:

"Mom, I know that you would like me to see you more often. When you express this to me, you either criticize me or try to make me feel guilty. This hurts me and makes me want to see you less. If you would express your feelings in a kinder format, it would be easier for me to give you what you want."

The elements used in this example are: acknowledgment of motive, cause and effect with regard to how the person in the example is affected by their mother's behavior, and then offering a viable solution. It is then up to their loved one to decide how to address this issue: whether they can resolve this on their own or whether they need professional help.

TAKE A MINDFUL MINUTE

Raising these issues with loved ones is difficult and stressful and may induce fear if there is a history of abuse. It is important that you monitor your stress and take breaks, when necessary, as high levels of stress are very bad for your health.

I suggest trying different self-care techniques. Many people find meditation helpful. You might use this opportunity to reflect on your limits and boundaries, and acknowledge that you are speaking to your loved one with the intention of improving the relationship, even though you may get feedback that is different. This will keep you more focused and centered.

Do something nice for yourself as a reward for championing the relationship even though your loved one may be resistant. This can take the form of a massage, walk, workout, nap, etc. Be generous with yourself when it comes to taking care of your feelings.

Key Takeaways

- BPD symptoms cause difficulties in relationships with loved ones.

- Understanding how BPD affects the ways in which your loved one relates to you is critical in improving the relationship.

- You will need to set boundaries in order to protect yourself from hurtful behavior patterns that are associated with BPD symptoms.

- The future of the relationship is largely dependent on your loved one's ability to partner with you against the symptoms of the disease.

3 How Your Relationship Affects You

Almost all humans crave the closeness, security, and sharing that come from intimate relationships. In order to achieve this, we must expose more of ourselves to others. With this exposure comes vulnerability to being hurt. Individuals we are intimately attached to can hurt us more than people we are not attached to because we care more about what they think and feel about us and how they treat us.

BPD symptoms cause instability in relationships. This effect is most significant in intimate relationships, though it affects people in all types of relationships, from siblings to co-workers to friends. In this chapter, you will learn about how various BPD symptoms disrupt your relationship. ●

The Experience of Loving Someone with BPD

Relationships are fundamentally dynamic. They are molded by the collection of experiences a person has, and by each interaction that you have with each individual. Expressing anger in relationships with intimate partners pushes them away and decreases intimacy. Kindness or empathy draws them closer and increases intimacy.

Individuals who suffer from symptoms of BPD have unstable moods, and that makes their behavior unstable. Individuals with loved ones who have BPD experience constant pushing and pulling, as constructive behaviors are interlaced with destructive ones. You can have an intimate relationship with someone with BPD, but until they stabilize themself, the relationship will also be unstable.

Instability causes anxiety, while stability induces security and tranquility. Much of your anxiety associated with your relationship is due to the fact that your loved one's behavior seems unpredictable. This causes you to be very cautious in your approach to your loved one and has been described as "walking on eggshells."

The most satisfying relationships are secure. These relationships require a high level of consistency in how each person treats and responds to the other person. They are reliable and predictable. The core of the relationship is based on such consistency and security that daily transactions have a limited effect on the relationship overall.

Insecure attachments occur frequently when symptoms of BPD are present. The relationship is reactive to every transaction. The relationship is defined largely based on the last transaction, rather than the overall history of transactions.

Being in an insecure intimate relationship will increase your overall stress level. For this reason, it is very important that you monitor your stress level. People experience stress in different ways. Some people experience stress directly, for example, as feeling tense, keyed up, or anxious. Others experience stress somatically in the form of headache, stomachache, loss of appetite, difficulty sleeping, etc. And others don't directly experience the stress at all, but it affects their health negatively, such as with high blood pressure or a weakened immune system. Knowing how you experience stress will help you monitor your stress, which is the first step toward management.

Managing your stress also means managing your stress-related behaviors. Examples include habitual use of substances, binge eating, overexercising, and workaholism. If you are using these types of behaviors to cope with your intimate relationship, then the relationship is making you sick. When this happens, you must modify the relationship.

This section looks at how some of the key features of BPD affect your relationship with your affected loved one, and how this might be affecting you.

THE EMOTIONAL ROLLER COASTER

The emotional dysregulation often present in individuals suffering from symptoms of BPD makes for extreme highs and lows in intimate relationships. Highs can turn into lows very quickly based on a single transaction. Jenna experienced this with her partner, Nadine, who experiences symptoms of BPD.

Jenna met Nadine at yoga class. She was attracted to her right away, and Nadine was very friendly and a good listener, so they decided to have dinner later in the week. They had a lovely dinner, and afterward Nadine invited Jenna up to her apartment for a drink.

It was very unlike Jenna to open up so quickly, but Nadine seemed to really see who she was. They spent the night together, and in the morning Jenna expected to continue the warmth and closeness from the night before. Nadine was already up and dressed for the day when Jenna woke up. She had a stern look on her face, and they had the following conversation.

NADINE: We need to talk.

JENNA: Sure, what's up?

NADINE: About last night.

JENNA: I had a great time.

NADINE: Well, I didn't.

JENNA: I thought you were happy.

NADINE: I was. But you didn't even kiss me goodnight. I felt used.

JENNA: I fell asleep. I dreamed about you.

NADINE: Well, I didn't sleep at all. I don't think I can be your friend.

Jenna was crushed. She got her belongings and went home and cried all day. To her surprise, Nadine called in the evening. Her voice was bright, and she asked Jenna if she wanted to go out on Saturday. Jenna was stunned. She felt like a fool. But she decided to meet with Nadine on Saturday to talk about what had happened.

When Nadine showed up on Saturday, she brought a bottle of wine. She was radiant and affectionate. Jenna was completely confused. She asked Nadine if she was angry with her, but Nadine said that she couldn't wait to get together again. Jenna had a lovely evening with Nadine, but this push-pull pattern of relating continued, and Jenna's life began to feel like a roller coaster.

Nadine really liked Jenna from the moment she met her. She was very excited to have a new friend and immediately felt like she had known Jenna all her life. She was different from the other friends that Nadine had who got close to her and then abandoned her. She felt safe with Jenna.

The first night together was sheer bliss. But then Nadine began to feel like Jenna had started acting like all the others she had been with. She just rolled over and went to sleep. She pushed Jenna away in the morning because she anticipated that Jenna would leave her. So she left Jenna first.

She expected Jenna to apologize and beg her to give the relationship a chance. When Jenna didn't do that, Nadine felt worthless. This confirmed to her that Jenna was not really into her. She thought about calling Jenna to give her a piece of her mind. She thought about hurting herself, which would relieve the pain of feeling worthless. But she had to go to work. By lunchtime, she felt very sad and lonely. She missed having someone to talk to. She missed Jenna.

By the time she got home, she felt so empty that she couldn't think about anything except how much she wanted to be with someone. She needed to be with someone. So she called Jenna.

IMPULSIVITY

Impulsivity is behavior driven by feelings (impulses) more than thought. These impulses can be associated with internal sensations such as hunger, fatigue, thoughts, dreams, etc., or they can be triggered by environmental sensations such as food smells, seeing attractive people, driving by a mall or casino, etc. The infinite potential triggers make impulsive behavior unpredictable, which causes stress for loved ones.

JJ loves his sister Cait, but the thought of being with her made him anxious. Their father described Cait as "a loose cannon." She was frequently late to appointments and sometimes didn't show up at all. She had good intentions, but if something interested her, she went with it, and this often happened when they were supposed to meet. JJ often had meals alone in restaurants when Cait didn't show up for dinners or lunches.

Cait was a lot of fun to be with, but sometimes her behaviors in public made JJ uncomfortable. For example, if she found someone attractive, she let them know with seductive behavior. It didn't matter whether the person was single or not. If she felt warm, she would take off clothing no matter who was around. She did this around JJ's friends, and it embarrassed him.

Cait was also irresponsible with money. She would show up to a restaurant broke because on the way to the meal she saw a piece of jewelry or a trinket that she "just had to have," and JJ would get stuck with the bill. He often felt in a bind as she would ask to borrow money, which never got paid back.

What troubled JJ the most was Cait's impulsive angry outbursts. She had no filter. If she had a thought or a feeling, she would express it no matter where they were or who was around. If she felt disrespected or slighted, she would curse at the person no matter who they were. Sometimes these outbursts were targeted at JJ.

JJ tried to talk to Cait about his discomfort with her impulsive behavior. He told her that he loved her and loved spending time with her but that he found it stressful due to the unpredictability of her behavior. She stated that she did not think that she did anything wrong.

HOW YOUR LOVED ONE MIGHT FEEL

Cait loved her brother very much. He was very supportive during her gender transition, and she was very grateful, but she felt that he just doesn't get her. She sees herself as a "free spirit." She is proud of her body and sees no reason why she should hide it or not share it.

She considers herself artistic, expressive, and quirky, and is proud of these features. She speaks her mind to others and figures it is their problem if they are offended. She didn't understand why JJ blamed her when other people didn't like what she said.

Cait also didn't understand why JJ was so uptight about being on time for appointments, but that was his problem to deal with. She also saw him as very tight with his money and untrusting, but she figured that was his insecurity and had nothing to do with her. She would like to see more of her brother, but she had to be herself.

FEAR OF ABANDONMENT

The fear of abandonment that is often present in individuals who suffer from symptoms of BPD causes a different type of stress. For loved ones of these individuals, there is a persistent need to demonstrate that they are available and present. For Freddie, this became a constant burden that caused him stress throughout the day.

Freddie is thirty-seven years old and married. Ever since he was a child, his mother, Selma, insisted on knowing where he was at all times. She also expected him to call her each morning and evening to check in, no matter what he was doing or where he was. If she didn't hear from him, she would make comments like "Did you forget you had a mother?" Every time he heard this from her, it was like getting kicked in the stomach. He did everything she asked of her, and if it wasn't done exactly her way, she accused him of being a bad person or a bad son.

Sometimes Freddie's mother would call him, and if he didn't pick up the phone, she would say that she had to speak to him right away. Each time she called, Freddie would drop everything and call her back. Sometimes she didn't pick up. Sometimes she would ask something that was not urgent, like "Which cable provider do you use?" This left Freddie feeling like a fool, but he was afraid to not respond in case there was some sort of emergency.

Freddie tried a few times to discuss this with her, but she never apologized. Instead, she got defensive. She would make statements like "I understand. I am just not that important to you. You have your life, and I am not a part of it."

What Freddie dreaded the most was the way she behaved when he traveled. She made him feel guilty for *leaving her*. On two occasions, she told him that she "might not still be around" when he returned because "no one cares whether I live or die."

Freddie tried so hard not to dwell on this and be present for his family if he was on vacation, or for his colleagues if he was away on business. But his mother's persistent clinginess ruined every trip for him.

HOW YOUR LOVED ONE MIGHT FEEL

Selma has been single for twenty years and she lives alone. Every day is a challenge for her. She feels completely isolated, like nobody would even know if she dropped off the face of the earth.

She feels better while she is working as she is around other people, but she needs to hear from Freddie before and after work. She figures that is not too much to ask. After all, she gave birth to him and raised him.

Selma is envious of other women her age. They all look happy and secure with husbands, children, and grandchildren all around them. She doesn't understand why they have such good luck and she has bad luck. She wonders why Freddie and his wife don't ask her to come live with them. They have room in their house. Selma is angry and resentful about this. She doesn't confront Freddie directly, but she can't help it that barbed comments sometimes slip out.

She would love to have other people in her life, but she has given up trying to find someone to be close with because they all inevitably let her down. Freddie is the only one she can absolutely rely on, and even he frequently disappoints her.

SUICIDAL OR SELF-MUTILATING BEHAVIOR

Threats and acts of self-harm take on many different forms in sufferers of BPD and are done for many different reasons. In some situations, these gestures can threaten significant damage or even death, so they must be taken seriously. In the following story, Sheila and her husband, Randall, came to fear for the life of their daughter, Harriet.

Harriet was an anxious child and often fussed with her body. She frequently pulled at her hair, bit her nails, and scratched at her skin, particularly when feeling uncomfortable, which was most of the time. Her parents corrected her sometimes, but other times they just let her do it because she would whine if they stopped her. They were not overly concerned, and neither was her pediatrician.

As Harriet entered puberty, Sheila began to notice frequent cuts and scratches on Harriet's body. She mentioned this to Harriet, who explained that it had occurred during gym class. After Sheila had mentioned this several times to Harriet, the scratches became less apparent.

When Harriet was a high school junior, Sheila entered her room one day without knocking, because she thought that Harriet was out. She was shocked to see Harriet cutting herself with a razor. She saw that Harriet had not stopped self-mutilating, she just did it on parts of her body that could be easily covered by clothing.

From that day on, Harriet became more overt about her self-harm. When her parents said no to her, she threatened to hurt or kill herself, or she cut herself in a spot they could observe. They generally gave in to her when she did this, fearing that if they didn't, she would hurt herself badly.

One time she cut too deep and couldn't stop the bleeding. She had to get stitches at the local emergency room. The doctor there asked her how she got the wound. Harriet lied and said that she had broken a glass by mistake and got cut.

Harriet is now 23, but still lives with her parents. Randall and Sheila live in constant fear that Harriet will hurt herself badly. They are afraid to leave her alone. They are afraid to say no to her and so they give in to her every demand. They feel trapped and helpless.

HOW YOUR LOVED ONE MIGHT FEEL

Harriet thinks that everybody is making too big a deal about her cutting. They don't seem to understand that the drawing of blood gives her tranquility when she is most agitated from within, and she has given up trying to explain it to them.

When people disrespect her or ignore her—or worse, when they abandon her—she truly starts to feel like life is not worth living. She is not "threatening self-harm." She is simply telling them how she feels. They are making her feel this way and they can either do something about it or not. As far as Harriet is concerned, this is up to them, and she will respond naturally. If they continue to hurt her, she will have no choice but to hurt herself.

She gets very annoyed when her dad reminds her about the time she cut too deep and had to go to the hospital for stitches. Everyone makes a mistake from time to time. She thinks to herself, *They should know that I know better now. I know what I am doing.*

ANGER

Inappropriate, intense anger or difficulty controlling anger causes fear in loved ones of individuals who suffer from BPD. It causes them to over-scrutinize everything they say and do and everything they don't say and don't do. This is what is referred to as "walking on eggshells."

Cassie had a very difficult decision to make. She loved her boyfriend, Jorge, but she did not feel safe around him. Most of the time, he was kind, loving, and fun to be with, but when he felt that others were slighting him, or going against him in any way, he lashed out angrily.

One night she canceled a date with him because she was feeling under the weather. She could see him on FaceTime as his face tightened, and his voice sounded like someone was choking him. He told her, "Go **** yourself" and then hung up the phone.

She was devasted. She felt like he was not the person she thought she knew. She was surprised when he called the next day and asked to see her as if nothing had happened.

This is when Jorge explained to Cassie that he had been neglected as a child and got triggered by rejection. She told him that it frightened her and he told her not to worry, and that he was in control.

She did start seeing him again, but she worried. Cassie noticed that Jorge lashed out at others as well. One time they were in a restaurant, and someone banged into Jorge accidently and spilled his drink. Jorge grabbed the guy by the cuffs of his shirt and was going to hit him. Management stepped in and asked them to leave.

When Cassie asked Jorge about his behavior in the restaurant, he stated that it was the other guy's fault for not being more careful. She began to wonder if he was capable of hurting someone. Maybe her. He was not reassuring.

Jorge hated when Cassie brought up his aggression. He didn't think it was abnormal, but rather saw himself as "doing what a man has to do to be a man." His father taught him that. Besides, he was never aggressive with anyone that didn't try to hurt him first. Therefore, he was justified in his behavior. It was their fault for starting with him.

He really didn't like being forced to leave the restaurant with Cassie just because some jerk spilled something on him. He was the victim, and he got punished! If Cassie had not been there, he would have given that manager a piece of his mind. Early Sunday morning, Jorge went to the dog park in town and collected a bag of dog poop and left the bag on the front door of the restaurant for the manager to find when he opened for business. He figured that would teach him not to mess with Jorge!

WRITE IT DOWN

Each of the behavior patterns, or dynamics, described in the previous scenarios causes stress in different ways to loved ones of individuals with symptoms of BPD. You will have to weigh the stress associated with the relationship against the pleasures of the relationship.

Make a list of the behavior patterns that affect you. Give each pattern a stress score from 1 to 10, with 1 being minimally stressful and 10 being intolerable. This will allow you to create a stress quotient by adding together the stress scores. The higher your stress quotient, the higher the price that you pay to be in the relationship. Stress quotients in double or triple digits may threaten your health and should be viewed as a warning sign that some changes need to be made or you will get sick staying in this relationship.

TAKE A MINDFUL MINUTE

Looking at an intimate relationship as being potentially bad for your health is a sobering thought. Take a moment to reflect on the fact that you cannot be in a healthy relationship if you are not healthy, and you can't be healthy if the relationship makes you sick. Take some deep breaths and focus on what you need from a relationship to add to your wellness.

Key Takeaways

- BPD symptoms cause behavior patterns in sufferers that have a significant effect on all of their intimate relationships and some casual ones as well.

- These relationship patterns, or dynamics, cause significant suffering to those who love them.

- The suffering that is caused by those with BPD symptoms can make loved ones sick.

- Relationship patterns that make you sick must either change or end. Someone who loves you does not want you to suffer.

4 How You Can Support Your Loved One

There are things you can do to support your loved one with symptoms of BPD and also things you should never do. First, you must support yourself. Just as the flight attendant tells you to put the oxygen mask on yourself before your child, you must protect your mental and physical health first or you will be of no use to anybody else. Continually allowing your loved one to hurt you hurts them, because it is enabling unhealthy behavior.

As you read on, keep in mind that support is not the same as *fixing*, *healing*, or *curing* them. You cannot do any of those, and you will fail if you try. Your loved one must take it upon themself to seek healing and growth, and then they will benefit from your support. Your loved one has to be the driver.

This is not going to be easy. Individuals with symptoms of BPD often get offended when they are told that there is something wrong with them. Later in this chapter, you will learn how to gently introduce this idea to your loved one. ●

Treatment of BPD

There is not one single or standard treatment for BPD. Several different approaches are targeted at different aspects of the disorder, and the optimal treatment is usually a combination of therapies. With the following treatments, BPD symptoms can be managed over time so they are less likely to significantly hinder one's life and relationships, but this requires making treating the disorder the primary focus of one's life.

Pharmacological treatment of BPD is complex and should only be done by psychiatrists with training in medicating individuals with BPD. No medication exists that treats BPD specifically, but many studies have found that psychiatric medications can be helpful in treating the various symptoms of BPD (Mercer et al., 2009).

There are two basic types of **psychotherapy**: behavioral and insight-oriented. They both can be useful in treating different aspects of the disorder in individuals suffering from symptoms of BPD.

- **Cognitive behavioral therapy (CBT)** involves helping individuals gain a greater level of control over their behavior by identifying thoughts that drive unwanted behaviors and then changing or blocking those thoughts. CBT may be a good choice to help individuals who self-harm by redirecting their thoughts to other behaviors that accomplish healthier reactions. For example, when thoughts of self-loathing lead to self-harm, these thoughts can be identified and responded to with self-soothing, such as a bath, instead.

- **Dialectical behavioral therapy (DBT)** was developed specifically for treatment of BPD (Linehan, 2015). DBT is a structured therapeutic approach that focuses on the way emotions are experienced and expressed. There are four core modules: mindfulness, distress tolerance, emotional regulation, and interpersonal relationships.

- **Insight-oriented psychotherapy** involves the therapist helping patients gain better insight into why they do what they do and the effects of their behaviors on others. This type of therapy is very effective with individuals who have symptoms of BPD, but many have difficulty tolerating it, because it requires that they identify personal weaknesses and take responsibility for correcting them. This format is necessary for optimal results when doing couples therapy or family therapy with an individual who has symptoms of BPD.

Residential treatment centers (RTCs) offer a setting other than the patient's home to treat moderate to severe cases of BPD. This modality is chosen when the person cannot be kept safe in their home environment or when they are destructive to others in their home. RTCs offer all of the other treatments listed on pages 52–53 in a concentrated setting. Individuals usually spend 30 to 90 days in the facilities and then go to transitional programs before returning to their home environment.

Encouraging Your Loved One to Seek Help

The following section applies mainly to loved ones who are adult sufferers of BPD symptoms. If your loved one is a minor, such as your child, you need to compel them to seek treatment.

Naturally, you want to encourage your loved one to seek professional help. Treatment can benefit both your loved one and your relationship, although it can be very difficult because they are likely to hear it as you saying that they are flawed or defective, which increases their self-loathing. This may lead to them either acting defensively or lashing out, at you or at themself, or both.

If you do decide to suggest to your loved one with symptoms of BPD that they get treatment, you should prepare for the worst but hope for the best. The following strategies and techniques will help increase the probability of a beneficial outcome.

TIMING

The instability of mood, identity, behavior, and relationships that are characteristic of BPD symptoms makes timing an important factor. Ask yourself, *when is my loved one most likely to be able to hear my suggestion in a loving and constructive way?* Many people are reluctant to bring up something potentially provocative when their loved one is in a good mood, but the alternative is to approach them when they are already agitated or defensive, during which your effort is bound to fail. The topic should be specifically avoided when your loved one shows any of the following features:

- **Victim identity.** It is very common for individuals suffering from symptoms of BPD to perceive themselves as a victim and blame others for undesirable aspects of their lives. Suggestions about treatment will increase their sense of being a victim, and they will probably blame you for not recognizing their mistreatment by others.

- **Expressions of self-loathing.** When your loved one shares that they are feeling empty or desperate or hopeless, you empathetically feel their pain. Similarly, when they are harming themself or talking about wanting to die, you naturally feel compelled to make a suggestion that might reduce their suffering: treatment. This suggestion is not likely to be constructively received at this time. More likely, they will get angry and accuse you of calling them crazy.

- **Expressions of anger.** The intense expressions of anger that most individuals with symptoms of BPD suffer are almost always associated with victim identity or self-loathing or both. Your suggestion about treatment will very likely increase their anger and target it your way.

If your suggestion of treatment is rejected by your loved one, the topic will probably become offensive to them, and any future efforts to bring it up will be much more likely to be rejected out of hand. Choose your timing carefully and approach them while they are in a relatively good mood.

DEFINE WHAT IS BROKEN

BPD is a personality disorder. Telling your loved one that you think they are afflicted is like telling them that their very sense of self is defective, which would be hurtful for anyone to hear. Your loved one will be more receptive if you define the problem as their mood or anxiety level, not them personally. This allows you to focus on relief for them from their suffering.

DO NOT PERSONALIZE IT

Rather than telling your loved one that you think they are sick and need professional help, you can bring up treatment for things that bother them in an impersonal, non-accusatory way. For example: "I read an article today about available remedies for depression (or anxiety, stress, insomnia, etc.) and people seem to be getting significant relief." You don't need to add: ". . . and I think you would benefit." They can figure this out for themself.

Even if you don't get the response you want from them immediately, they will likely give it some thought later and may come to a healthier conclusion.

TALK ABOUT IT

The proper delivery of your suggestion is so important that it is often helpful to create a script and perhaps rehearse it.

Ray loved Greta more than he had ever loved anyone, and she showed him more love than anyone ever had. But she was not able to do so consistently. Sometimes she told him how lucky she was to be with him, and other times she told him that he was a *loser* and she deserved to be with a *real man*. This hurt him to the core. He knew that the lashing out had more to do with her mood than his behavior, but it still hurt.

He tried to speak to her about this, but she just responded, "I am hurt, too." He figured if her mood was more stable, her behavior toward him would be as well. He waited until after they shared a lovely weekend away. When they returned, he initiated the following conversation.

RAY: I had a wonderful weekend. Thank you
so much.

GRETA: Me too.

RAY: I wish it could always be this way.

GRETA: Life is not one big vacation.

RAY: I asked my friend Bobby how he and Irene are
able to maintain closeness and tranquility
even when they are not on vacation.

GRETA: And what did he say?

RAY: He said that he used to experience mood
swings that affected their relationship. He
snapped at her and she would avoid him for
a few days until he returned to his calmer
state. He read an article about how some
people have chemical imbalances in their
brains that cause them to be sometimes
moody. He made an appointment with a
psychiatrist who put him on some medication, and he felt much better. He and Irene
both emphasized how much this helped
their relationship become more secure and
more intimate.

Ray should be prepared for Greta to ask the question, "So you think I have a chemical imbalance in
my brain?" This would be best answered, "I am not a
doctor, so I am not in a position to answer that, but
anything that might help you or us in any way is something I am interested in supporting."

Unfortunately, individuals with BPD are acutely sensitive to the perception that they are "crazy," and this is often what they feel is being implied when professional help is suggested. Even the indirect method described in the previous scenario risks them perceiving an implication that there is something wrong with them. They feel attacked by this and respond by either lashing out or by withdrawing.

Because many individuals with symptoms of BPD experience persistent self-loathing, it is very painful for them to be told that they should seek help, especially by a loved one. They may become defensive and seek to invalidate your opinion, not because you are wrong, but because it is painful.

What If Your Loved One Won't Seek Help?

Most people seek help when they experience significant pain or dysfunction. If your loved one refuses to seek help, the first thing you need to do is consider whether you are enabling them not to seek help by tolerating behaviors that are unhealthy for you and your loved one and that negatively impact the relationship. Lashing out, threats of self-harm, and impulsivity are examples.

In many situations, people are not aware that they are enabling their loved ones to not seek help. Consider the following.

Lee loves Cory very much but is considering ending the relationship. Cory is loving most of the time, but when frustrated he can lash out at Lee. The first time this happened, Lee was stunned. He told Cory that he could not tolerate the name-calling and screaming during these outbursts because he felt unsafe. Cory promised that it would not happen again.

But it did happen again. Lee again stated how it made him feel and reiterated that he would not tolerate it. The third time it happened, Lee demanded that Cory get treatment for an "anger problem." Cory refused. This pattern kept repeating but Lee stayed.

By not leaving Cory and repeatedly tolerating the lashing out, Lee was enabling Cory to avoid treatment. Had he refused to see Cory again until treatment was sought, it might have motivated Cory to seek help.

If your loved one refuses to get help, you must set boundaries that prevent those behaviors from continuing. For example, if your loved one humiliates you in public with inappropriate comments or behaviors and they can't stop on their own, then you need to stop going to public settings with them until they seek help to address their problem.

When setting boundaries, the goal should never be that they seek a particular treatment, or even treatment in general. The goal is they have to stop the harmful behavior. The reason for this is that going to treatment is desirable, but not enough. Your loved one must be engaged and fully participate until success is achieved. They must own the outcome, not just the process.

Your discussion with your loved one about their refusal to seek professional help for their issues that affect your relationship should be structured in a cause-and-effect format. In the following example, Fran asks her mother to refrain from blurting out personal comments in public. Her mother argues that she does not feel that there is anything wrong with her questions. Fran is concerned about her mother's behavior at her son's upcoming wedding.

> **FRAN:** Can you please speak to someone about your making impulsive comments in public? I am concerned that it might make Sonny and Sammy uncomfortable at their wedding.

> **MOM:** I told you that I don't think there is anything wrong with my questions and comments. The problem is that you are a prude. Maybe you should see a shrink.

> **FRAN:** Last week, you asked me if I was in menopause in front of my son's future in-laws. When you said that, I was mortified.

> **MOM:** I can't help it if your son's in-laws are repressed like you.

> **FRAN:** Mom, I really want to include you in my life, but comments like this embarrass me and make me not want you at these events. You won't be invited to Sonny and Sammy's wedding if you can't promise me that you'll work on this.

In this example, Fran made two attempts to express her thoughts and feelings in the cause-and-effect format. The final statement sets up the boundary: If Mom doesn't stop, she will have to be excluded from certain events in the future.

What to Do If Your Loved One Is Self-Harming or Suicidal

Self-harming, such as cutting or burning, pulling out hair, etc. as well as suicidal threats and gestures such as taking large amounts of medication or threatening to kill themselves, are very common in individuals who suffer from BPD. Researchers estimate that 65 to 80 percent (Soloff et al., 1994; Lieb et al., 2004) of individuals with BPD self-harm. About 9 percent of those diagnosed with BPD die by suicide (Zanarini et al., 2005). All behaviors or threats of self-harm or suicide must be taken seriously.

The first thing you should do if your loved one self-harms is to determine if they need immediate medical attention. The following are some signs, but this list is not exhaustive:

- Unconsciousness

- Uncontrolled bleeding

- Infected wound, particularly if accompanied by fever

- Cognitive dysfunction, such as difficulty speaking or walking

- Severe stomach pain or vomiting blood

If your loved one has any of these symptoms, or other signs of a severe medical condition, you must see to it that they get immediate medical attention.

If your loved one does not need immediate medical attention, then you should determine whether their self-harm was intentional or accidental. If you determine, or even suspect, that their self-harm was intentional, then you should do everything in your power to get them to see a mental health professional as soon as possible.

If your loved one is a minor and you are the parent, you must force them to see a mental health provider. If your loved one is an adult, you do not have this option, so you will have to try to persuade them. If this doesn't work, you might have to set a boundary that you cannot continue to spend time with someone who chooses to hurt themself.

The first thing you should do if your loved one threatens suicide is to determine if the threat is genuine. You do this by asking them. When doing this, it is best to let them know what will happen if they say yes. For example, "Are you telling me that you are seriously thinking of taking your life? Because if that's how you feel, I have to call an ambulance and get you to a hospital to keep you safe."

If they still insist that they are serious, then that means they want you to call an ambulance or take them to the hospital, and you should do so.

If they indicate that they are not serious about taking their life but they are trying to tell you how badly they feel, then you should say something like "I am interested in how you feel and I appreciate your sharing it with me, but if you are not serious about hurting yourself, then you need to express it differently. Just say you feel awful. If you say you are suicidal, I will see that you get to a hospital."

In this way, you convey to your loved one that you will respond in a loving and responsible way to their threats, which is seeing that they get urgent medical care, but that they should not use that language if they don't mean it.

The Limits of Support

The following section applies mainly to loved ones who are adult sufferers of BPD symptoms. If your loved one is a minor, such as your child, you need to compel them to seek treatment.

You cannot heal your loved one and you cannot force them to heal themself. If your loved one is trying to help themself, you can support this process.

You are not responsible for your loved one, though they might claim that you are. It is common for individuals with symptoms of BPD to make statements such as "If you don't visit with me today, I will kill myself," thus trying to make you responsible for their life. In this chapter, you learned what to do if threats like this are made. The decision to hurt themselves is theirs, not yours. The reality is that if someone really wants to hurt or kill themself, they probably will not announce it first—they will just do it.

Being in a relationship with this level of volatility can be very draining. Many in this position report being "exhausted" by it. This is because almost all intimate relationships with individuals with symptoms of BPD are highly transactional, or defined by the last interaction rather than the stability that naturally comes from shared history and experience.

You will have to assess whether the increase in stress associated with maintaining an intimate relationship with an individual with symptoms of BPD is worth the price you pay. If you decide that it is, your focus on self-care is paramount. Individuals with symptoms of BPD generally have weak empathy, which means that they are not reliable in their ability to take care of you. You are responsible for taking care of you.

TAKE A MINDFUL MINUTE

You knew that something was different in your relationship with a loved one with BPD. Now you understand that this relationship requires extra effort on your part and significant sacrifices as compared to a secure relationship that you might have with someone who does not suffer from symptoms of BPD.

A key factor is how you cope with the additional stress and sacrifices. This determines the cost of being in the relationship. Take some time to take inventory of what your actual price is. Does it affect your health? Your work? Your ability to have sanctuary in the relationship or in your home? You need to minimize this price. Does your loved one cooperate with these efforts?

People who love you don't want you to have to suffer to be with them. They don't want you to suffer at all. Take a moment to reflect on what your life would be like without your loved one with symptoms of BPD.

Key Takeaways

- Many treatments are available to individuals with symptoms of BPD.

- These treatments are beneficial for management of the disorder, but they require consistency.

- These treatments are largely ineffective if your loved one with BPD symptoms does not cooperate and fully participate.

- You can provide support, but your ability to help is limited.

- You must monitor how you are affected by the stress and sacrifices associated with loving an individual with symptoms of BPD.

5 Helping You and Your Loved One Manage BPD

All relationships are developed, defined, and maintained through patterns of communication and are affected by all types: what is said, what is not said, how it is said, and how people behave toward each other.

Form is how information is transferred between two people; *content* is the information itself. Examples of form include: respectful, defensive, challenging, demeaning, insulting, abusive, etc. These qualities can be present regardless of content. Examples of content include: where to have dinner, decisions about shared children (coparenting), where to go on vacation.

This chapter will help you understand more completely your communication patterns with your loved one with BPD and how they shape your relationship. We will focus on how to modify some of these patterns to decrease conflict and increase closeness in your relationship. ●

Communication

Spontaneous communication, just saying what you think or feel, requires minimal effort but affords little control. This type of communication should be reserved only for the most intimate and secure relationships. In the context of an insecure attachment, which characterizes most relationships that are affected by significant symptoms of BPD, spontaneous communication will not produce the best results, and can lead to conflict and hurt.

MINDFUL COMMUNICATION

If your loved one has symptoms of BPD, you will have the best outcome using mindful communication. This means thinking about what you say and how you say it before you say anything. This requires much more effort than spontaneous communication but produces better and more predictable results.

Some criticize this approach as being manipulative. Manipulation can be done for loving purposes or for deceptive ones. We will be dealing only with benevolent manipulation—that which is done for the purpose of benefiting the relationship and helping your loved one manage symptoms of BPD.

First, you must differentiate between healthy and unhealthy communication. Healthy communication increases intimacy while respecting the individual needs and sensitivities of both participants. Unhealthy communication does not do this, and it undermines efforts to increase intimacy, resulting in resentment, conflict, stress, anxiety, and alienation.

FORM BEFORE CONTENT

Assess the form of the conversation before you attend to the content. You should only address content that is presented ideally in a respectful form, but you must insist that it at least be civil. In the following example, Zoe is using mindful communication to help Joy reap the benefits of healthy communication.

JOY: Zoe, how could you be so stupid as to make a reservation for dinner at that horrible café?

ZOE: Can we talk about this calmly and respectfully?

JOY: I am calm, but you did a stupid thing.

ZOE: Speaking to me that way is disrespectful. If you would like to discuss dinner plans, please be respectful.

JOY: Don't give me that psychobabble. I am going to cancel it and make a different reservation.

ZOE: . . .

JOY: Did you hear what I said?

ZOE: I am only willing to discuss this with you respectfully. I am speaking respectfully to you.

This tool must be exercised consistently. If you make it clear that you won't respond to content that is offered disrespectfully, your loved one will be forced to either have healthy communication or not communicate. Noncommunication is less harmful to the relationship than unhealthy communication. If your loved one values the relationship, they will eventually acquiesce. Keep in mind that you are showing your loved one that respectful communication is more effective overall than disrespectful communication.

CONSCIOUS VS. UNCONSCIOUS COMMUNICATION

Conscious communication consists of intentional sharing of information, thoughts, feelings, and awareness of what is being communicated. This is largely what is said. Unconscious communication involves information that is gleaned from indirect cues that might not be intentionally offered. These include cues conveyed by vocal tone, body posture, how things are phrased, etc.

GERRY GETS AN OFFER HE CANNOT REFUSE

In the following dialogue, J.P., who suffers from symptoms of BPD, invites his close friend Gerry to go out to dinner on Friday.

J.P.: Gerry, how about we go for a movie and quick bite on Friday?

GERRY: I am sorry, J.P., Friday is not good for me.

J.P.: Why not?

GERRY: I already have plans.

J.P.: Oh. Obviously, someone you care about more than me.

GERRY: No. I just made the other plans first.

J.P.: I get it. I don't come first. I will go with somebody else.

GERRY: Do what you have to do. I didn't do anything wrong. I had plans.

J.P.: With who?

GERRY: What difference does it make?

J.P.: I just want to know.

GERRY: It's not important.

J.P.: Oh. So it is your secret friend.

GERRY: It's not a secret.

J.P.: Then why won't you tell me?

GERRY: Whatever!

Gerry became exasperated and ended the conversation. J.P. felt worthless and dismissed. His empathy failed him at that moment, and he was unable to see that Gerry was not trying to diminish the relationship but wanted to honor a prior commitment.

Gerry felt unfairly attacked by J.P. and hurt. It felt like J.P. was refusing to understand about the prior commitment and was very accusatory. Gerry was unsure about whether or not to continue the relationship.

WHAT COULD HAVE BEEN DONE DIFFERENTLY

Prevention: Individuals with BPD have a great sensitivity to abandonment. Because of this, they tend to listen *for* signs of abandonment, rather than listening *to* what is being said. Insecurity responds well to reassurance. Gerry might have avoided some of the conflict by responding to the invitation with reassurance while offering an alternative. For example: "I would love to do dinner and a movie with you, but I can't make it Friday. How about Saturday?"

Defensiveness: Once the conversation progressed, it became more conflictual, in part due to Gerry's defensiveness, such as the statement "I didn't do anything wrong." J.P. then felt he had to show that Gerry *was* doing something wrong and contrived the secret relationship.

Defensiveness should be replaced with validation. For example, "J.P., I know that you are disappointed that I can't make it Friday night, and I love to spend time with you, too. Let's go out either Saturday or Sunday."

Unconscious communication: J.P. talked about Friday evening and asked a lot of questions, but the unconscious message is "I am hurt and angry that you will not change your plans to spend Friday evening with me." This message is conveyed by his angry tone and his threat to go out with someone else.

If Gerry had identified the unconscious part of the communication, it would have presented an opportunity to address this central part of the communication. This might sound like "J.P., you are a dear friend, and I highly value our time together. I also really appreciate your flexibility in choosing times that are comfortable for both of us. How about Saturday?"

The more you can see patterns in the communication and behavior of your loved one, the more helpful you will be to them in managing BPD symptoms in your relationship. Recording these behaviors in your journal will allow you to see if ways of relating to you repeat over time. If so, you have identified a pattern that will allow you to formulate a consistent strategy that will be maximally effective at getting the relationship back on track.

In the previous example, we identified three ways of relating that are likely to be patterns, but we won't know until additional interactions confirm or disconfirm that these are actual patterned, or stable, ways of relating. These three potential patterns are:

- J.P. tends to listen for signs of abandonment rather than listening to what is being said.

- J.P. responds to defensiveness by attacking more.

- J.P. communicates certain emotions (hurt, or anger in this case) indirectly, or unconsciously.

Making notes such as the bullet points on page 25 in your journal will help you identify these patterns and respond most effectively. We will now discuss what some of your responses to these patterns might be.

Once you have identified unhealthy patterns of communication, discuss it with your loved one. If you don't discuss the pattern, you will have to respond every time this behavior occurs, and your loved one may feel like you have issues with everything they say. This will increase their self-loathing.

Confrontation is a primary tool you will need to use. When many people think of confrontation, they think of angry confrontation, often involving an ultimatum or threat of some sort. This is not the kind of confrontation being suggested here.

A gentle confrontation begins with an affirmation, such as "I really love you" or "our relationship is very important to me."

After the affirmation(s), you speak in a calm tone, and you present the pattern of unhealthy behavior in the context of your desire to make the relationship even better than it already is. Here is an example.

"I love spending time with you, and our relationship is extremely special and important to me. I wish you felt that as strongly as I feel so that you would not worry about my not valuing our relationship. I feel this way all of the time, even when I cannot be with you."

Generally, using gentle confrontation to let your loved one know that they are hurting you is less effective in dealing with individuals with symptoms of BPD, but is of some value nonetheless. You can do this in the cause-and-effect format discussed previously (page 60). The caution is that when you tell someone how to hurt you, you empower them to use this information to hurt you more. I will now give you some tools to manage this if it does occur.

Setting and Sticking to Boundaries

When your efforts to educate your loved one fail to garner cooperation in enhancing healthy communication, you will have to set and maintain boundaries that do not permit unhealthy communication.

Ideal functioning in intimate relationships occurs when there is maximum cooperation. Setting boundaries becomes an option only after cooperation has been attempted and failed. The hope is that eventually your boundaries are accepted, and your loved one is rewarded by your cooperating with them.

SELECTING BOUNDARIES

Crafting boundaries should be guided by whether behaviors are healthy or unhealthy to you, your loved one, and the relationship. Healthy behaviors should be encouraged and celebrated. Unhealthy behaviors are any behaviors that cause pain or dysfunction in either of you and discourage intimacy in your relationship.

Boundaries must be crafted so that you can effectively set and maintain them. Setting boundaries but not enforcing them makes things much worse.

MAINTAINING BOUNDARIES

There generally is little need to reinforce boundaries with healthy individuals. If you ask them not to smoke in your car, they are appreciative that you told them before they lit up, because they would feel bad if they smoked in your car without realizing that you don't like it.

Individuals with symptoms of BPD and other personality disorders test boundaries. Rather than honoring and respecting boundaries, they are offended by them. They object to them, so they violate them, sometimes overtly and defiantly. For example, when Jenny's father told her that she is not allowed to take the car out after 10 p.m. because she has a junior license, she grabbed the keys out of his hand at 10:30 and ran toward the garage.

Sometimes testing of boundaries is subtle. For example, Margie told her boyfriend, Sven, that she does not like PDA (public displays of affection). When they met Margie's parents for dinner at a nice restaurant, she reminded Sven that she did not like to be touched in public. As they were having dinner, he put his hand on her knee under the table. She brushed his hand off. He waited a few minutes and then replaced his hand. She brushed it off and then turned away. He then put his arm around her. She wiggled free and put her coat on. After dinner, she confronted him about his behavior, and he told her that nobody could see under the table, therefore it was not public.

When dealing with individuals who suffer from symptoms of BPD, it is critical that you enforce the boundaries you have set. If you do not, the unhealthy behaviors will increase in frequency and/or intensity. If Jenny's father does not enforce the 10 o'clock driving limitation, she will assume that she can drive whenever she wants. If Sven is not stopped from touching Margie in public, he will likely expand his range of PDA.

MOTHER KNOWS BEST, BUT GRANDMA WON'T LISTEN

Mandy was a single parent with two children, ages nine and eleven. She had to work full-time to support them, and her mother helped her with the kids after school and on weekends.

Mandy's children were both overweight due to poor diets. Their pediatrician told her that if they didn't get on a better diet and lose some weight, they would be at risk for developing diabetes. She decided to restrict their sugar intake, but the kids were not losing weight.

MANDY: Mom, are you giving the kids sugar while they are at your house?

MOM: A little sugar won't hurt them.

MANDY: Mom, they are overweight, and the doctor wants them to lose weight.

MOM: It's just baby fat.

MANDY: The children need to lose weight. Please don't give them sugar.

MOM: Well, I guess you are the mother, and I am just Granny.

A week later, Mandy caught her daughter, Lola, with a candy bar. She asked Lola where she got it. Lola told her Granny gave it to her but told her not to tell. Mandy was furious. She called her mother.

MANDY: Mom, I told you not to give the kids sugar.

MOM: I didn't.

MANDY: Then where did Lola get a candy bar from?

MOM: I guess she helped herself.

MANDY: If you don't stop giving the kids sugar, I won't leave them with you anymore.

A few days later, she caught her son, Mickey, with a cupcake. She was about to call her mother and tell her that she can't be left alone with the kids when she realized that she could not do that because she needed her mother to watch the kids when she was working. She was now in a bind.

WHAT COULD HAVE BEEN DONE DIFFERENTLY

The difficulty Mandy is having was set up by her relying on her mother for daily childcare. This is a form of codependency, where her dependency on her mother to take care of her children compromises her autonomy or ability to make decisions for herself and her children. Ideally, Mandy should have looked into other options for childcare, so as not to be dependent on her mother.

When Mandy asked her mother to cooperate with her decisions on the children's diet, her mother pushed back rather than accepting what Mandy asked. This happens frequently with individuals with BPD, as one of the symptoms is low frustration tolerance. She might have used the form-before-content tool by saying, "Mom, why are you opposing my efforts to make my children healthier?" The conversation then becomes about cooperating with Mandy's parenting decisions, rather than about sugar. Hopefully, Mandy's mom could express the unconscious part of the communication, which is that Granny will do anything to keep them interested in spending time with her. Mandy could then suggest other ways that her mom can keep the kids interested, such as taking up a mutual hobby.

Another option for Mandy is to educate her children about the health concerns raised by their doctor and convince them that it is in their best interest to refuse sugar when it is offered to them by Granny or by anyone else.

If none of these remedies work, Mandy will have to set boundaries with the children. She might tell them that if she catches them with sweets again, they will have to go from school to her workplace and wait for her to finish, instead of going home to Granny.

Individuals with symptoms of BPD are particularly sensitive to being told what to do. They are likely to experience this as feeling demeaned, which contributes to their feelings of self-loathing. Whenever possible, you should make requests rather than demands. Provide context so that your loved one feels like they are part of the process and not being directed. Mandy might have gotten a better response from her mother had she approached her like this:

MANDY: Mom, I just took the kids to their doctor. The doctor is concerned about their being overweight, which could lead to prediabetes.

MOM: Oh my. What can we do?

MANDY: We have to help them eat healthier.

MOM: Perhaps we should have them see a dietician.

MANDY: That is a great suggestion, but why don't we see what we can do for them first? They really love your cooking. Do you think you could come up with some recipes that would satisfy their sweet cravings with less sugar content?

MOM: I am happy to try.

Mandy is able to engage her mother by making her feel part of, and in fact vital, to the process. She offers Granny an opportunity to be creative with the children's diet, with the goal of lowering sugar intake, that honors her need to keep the children interested in spending time with her.

WHAT TO DO WHEN BOUNDARIES ARE CROSSED

Most individuals with symptoms of BPD react to boundaries by testing them: violating them to see if you will react. If you don't react, they will test more, so violating boundaries must have consequences.

Situation-specific consequences are applied only in a specific situation. If you asked someone you love not to embarrass you in public and they continue to do so, then the consequence is that you will not appear with them in public. The relationship otherwise stays the same.

Relationship-specific consequences apply to all aspects of the relationship across circumstances. Loss of trust is an example. If your loved one violates your boundaries frequently, then you will no longer trust them to behave respectfully and in your best interest. For example, Mandy might have said to her mother, "If I can't trust you to help me with the children's diet, then I don't see how I can trust you at all."

When setting relationship-specific consequences, follow-through is crucial. You need to bring up the issue of trust in multiple contexts. For example, if Granny offers to take the children to a movie, Mandy can state, "I would love to have you take the children to the movie, but I don't trust you to keep them away from unhealthy foods." This doesn't necessarily mean that Granny doesn't get to take the kids to the movie, but Mandy can insist on going along with them. Or Mandy can give the kids healthy snacks and tell them they can only go to the movie if they agree not to buy any snacks at the theater.

Replace Unhealthy Connection with Healthy Connection

Individuals with symptoms of BPD seek constant affirmation that they are important and that you will not leave them. This tends to cause the relationships to be codependent. Codependent relationships involve people doing things for each other that each should be doing for themselves. Examples include feeding a child who is capable of feeding himself. The parent enjoys feeding the child and likes the fact that the child will not be accustomed to eating without them. It also inhibits the child's confidence in his ability to feed himself.

Healthy connections are mutually respectful. They support independence and autonomy rather than codependency. They are fundamentally cooperative and not competitive.

UNHEALTHY CONNECTION	HEALTHY CONNECTION
Insecure	Secure
Unstable	Stable
Codependent	Independent/Autonomous
Competitive	Cooperative

Changing an unhealthy connection into a healthy connection is a process. You will have to consistently block unhealthy behavior patterns and replace them with healthy behavior patterns.

INSECURE ⟶ SECURE

The best way to make an insecure connection more secure is to offer frequent affirmation and reassurance. Tell your loved one often that you love them and love to be with them. Point out positive contributions that they make to the relationship and your life whenever possible and be specific.

UNSTABLE ⟶ STABLE

You increase the stability of the relationship by being consistent in your behavior toward your loved one. Speak in steady tones, especially during conflicts. Clearly express boundaries and reinforce them consistently.

CODEPENDENT ⟶ INDEPENDENT/ AUTONOMOUS

Codependent behavior patterns are formed when your loved one engages you in doing things for them that they should be able to do for themself. They often do this for reassurance that you will not abandon them and that they are worthy of attention. A common example is your being asked to remind them of things that they need to do, making you responsible for them doing these things.

Another common example of codependent behavior is when your loved one makes you responsible for their lives. They may threaten that if you don't do something for them or with them, they will hurt themself, making you responsible for whether or not they hurt themself.

Converting codependent connections into autonomous ones requires consistent refusal to participate in codependent patterns while offering healthy alternatives. For example, if your friend asks you to remind them to renew their driver's license, you might suggest that they do it now and not have to worry about it anymore.

COMPETITIVE ⟶ COOPERATIVE

Individuals with symptoms of BPD often see resources as limited, resulting in them routinely competing with loved ones for those resources. Competition for attention is very common, as is competition for more tangible resources such as an inheritance or the favor of a boss, teacher, or parent.

Competition is the opposite of cooperation. A good competitor does everything they can to undermine their opponent. This undermines closeness and trust and hence inhibits intimacy.

You should always refuse to compete with your loved ones and look for cooperative alternatives. For example, if your sister is competing with you for attention or affection from your parents, you should suggest ways that your parents will pay attention to both of you. If your sister made arrangements to pick up your parents at the airport without telling you so that she could be the one to greet them, rather than arguing with her, you can arrange to have a meal waiting for them when they get back from the airport.

Using one of these methods consistently will most likely make your relationship healthier. This will not cure your loved one but will improve the relationship that the two of you share.

OVERPARENTING: WHEN MOM DOES TOO MUCH

Throughout childhood, Sadie relied heavily on her parents for her daily functioning. In high school, her father had to wake her up every day and her mother had to take her to school, because she didn't like to go on the bus alone. Sadie got married when she was twenty-four and moved into an apartment with her husband right down the street from her mother, Sierra.

Sierra was very involved with Sadie when she got pregnant. She was around every day to help with doctor visits and keep the home clean. She also helped Sadie and her husband out financially on a monthly basis. This continued through three pregnancies. Sierra practically lived with her daughter as she was over there so frequently.

Six months ago, Sadie's husband left her. She was blindsided and distraught. She told her mother that she did not know if she could go on with her life all alone. Sadie said that she could not bear to live in the apartment without her husband and Sierra reluctantly agreed that she and the children could move in with her temporarily.

Sierra did enjoy having her grandchildren living with her but soon started to feel taken advantage of. Sadie did not offer to help in any way. Sierra shopped, cooked, and cleaned. Sadie and the children helped themselves to food and other supplies but did not clean up after themselves. Sadie also did not contribute financially to Sierra's home even though she was getting money from her ex-husband and social services.

After three months, Sierra asked Sadie when she might be finding a new apartment with the children and living independently. Sadie screamed at her, asking how she could abandon her child and grandchildren. She called her a terrible mother and threatened that if she and the children were forced to leave, Sierra would never see any of them ever again.

Sierra felt completely trapped. She had no life of her own because she spent all of her time taking care of her daughter and her grandchildren. Sadie demanded that Sierra be available for her and the kids all the time, but did not make efforts or progress to live independently, get a job, or take over parenting her children. Sierra found herself in a massive codependent gridlock.

WHAT COULD HAVE BEEN DONE DIFFERENTLY

The best interventions are those done in advance. Sierra should have been working with Sadie and her husband to gain full independence while they were still together and before the children were born. Instead of continuing to supplement their monthly income, she should have steadily reduced her financial support so that Sadie and her husband could be compelled to achieve full financial independence.

When Sadie got pregnant the first time, Sierra should have made clear what she was willing to do for them and what she was not willing to do. This is a type of boundary and requires a plan for reduction of support as Sadie and her family grew into their new circumstances. In not doing this, her daughter and son-in-law took advantage and allowed her to do things that they could have done for themselves, such as shopping, cooking, and cleaning the house.

By allowing Sadie and the kids to move in with her, Sierra was preventing them from adjusting to life as a single-parent household. This was another opportunity for Sierra to work with Sadie on a plan to use Sierra's help minimally, while striving toward increased independence as she healed from the divorce. Sierra will still have to make such a plan, but it will be much harder because Sadie and the kids are firmly enmeshed in a codependent family situation.

In order for your loved one to participate in a new and healthier connection, they must understand what you are trying to do. Maximum transparency will minimize your loved one's feelings of not being included and increase the opportunity for them to participate cooperatively.

When communicating your efforts to your loved one, you should use two of the tools we discussed earlier: affirmation/reassurance and context. Here is how Sierra might have discussed this with Sadie using these two tools.

"Sadie, although I am very sad that your marriage didn't work out, I have enjoyed spending extra time with you and the children. I think it is now time that we talk about moving forward toward healing by restoring your independence and autonomy. Of course, I will continue to help you and the children out in many ways, but perhaps we should discuss your finding a new apartment."

In this sample dialogue, Sierra begins and ends with affirmation and reassurance that she will still be a significant presence in Sadie's life while putting her finding a new apartment in the context of healing and growth.

Sierra will probably still have to deal with resistance and protest, but this is the first step. She may have to raise this issue multiple times. She should do so in as consistent a manner as possible.

Keeping track of your efforts to convert unhealthy connections and communications into healthy ones will help you maintain consistency in your approach. You can write down the specific behavior changes that you are instituting in areas of security, stability, independence, and cooperation. Each day, reflect on the behaviors of the day and note in your journal how the four areas of change are supported. The goal is for your behavior to become increasingly natural in the pursuit of a healthy connection, while eliminating behaviors of yours that enable unhealthy connection.

Make a Plan

You have learned in this chapter that the best approach to making your relationship with your loved one with BPD better is preemptive. The first step is to create a plan. Articulating specific goals and methods facilitates participation and cooperation, because it provides understanding and inclusion.

A relationship plan is often referred to as a *behavioral contract*. It is a document that articulates standards for healthy behaviors and consequences and remedies for unhealthy ones. The plan should have the following three components:

- Statement of goals

- Target behaviors

- Methods of achieving the goals

For example, one of the goals might be greater stability in the relationship. The target behavior might be conflict.

The method is to reduce conflict by using processes such as forgiveness, tolerance, compromise, and respect. The method section might also include an understanding that if conflicts escalate as you try to resolve them, you both agree to take a 24-hour break from the topic to let each of you cool down and reflect.

INTRODUCING THE PLAN TO YOUR LOVED ONE

It is essential that you introduce the idea of a plan to your loved one in such a way as to garner maximum cooperation. You should keep in mind that your loved one might not feel that there is anything wrong and therefore a plan is not needed. In this case, you will have to explain to them what you think could be improved, without complaining.

You should not bring your loved one a fully formed plan. This leaves them feeling that you are imposing the plan on them. You want them to feel that you are inviting them to participate in a venture with you with a mutual goal. Be willing to negotiate and compromise on methods and goals and show a willingness to add target behaviors that are important to them.

The behavioral contract is particularly important in relationships that are affected by BPD. The plan offers *security,* because it gives the relationship structure, definition, and boundaries. It encourages *stability*, because it offers a blueprint for consistent behavior patterns. It encourages *independence* and *autonomy*, because it holds each person responsible for their own behaviors and for taking actions to support the health of the relationship. It encourages and provides a medium for *cooperation* and the creation of mutual growth. Let's see how it's done.

THE BREAKUP/MAKEUP ROLLER COASTER

Cheri met Rho online through a dating site during the COVID-19 pandemic. They lived 1,000 miles apart, so they dated virtually for six months, then Rho invited Cheri to cohabitate on a trial basis, because Cheri was able to work from home. Once they started to live together, Cheri saw another side of Rho.

Cheri had only lived with Rho for one week when Rho got upset with her for being noisy in the morning and asked her to leave. As Cheri was packing in tears, Rho came back and told her not to leave. She expressed that asking Cheri to leave was just an expression of frustration. This happened several more times: seemingly good moments, followed by frustration, anger, and pain. Cheri started to see that there was a pattern.

Cheri was experiencing the emotional roller coaster described in chapter 3 (page 37). It made Cheri anxious all the time, and she was having difficulty focusing on her work. She decided that she needed to talk to Rho and come up with a plan that would lead to greater stability in the relationship. The next time they had an argument, they had the following dialogue.

> **CHERI:** I can't take it anymore.
>
> **RHO:** You can't take what anymore?
>
> **CHERI:** Your anger and threats.
>
> **RHO:** What anger and threats?
>
> **CHERI:** Like threatening to throw me out of your apartment.
>
> **RHO:** I told you I don't mean that. I just say it in the moment.

CHERI: I can tolerate your sharing your feelings of anger and frustration, but I can't tolerate them being directed at me that way. If you don't stop, I will have to leave.

RHO: Now you are threatening me.

CHERI: I am not threatening you. I am trying to set a boundary so that we can be closer to each other.

RHO: Setting a boundary and threatening to leave me if I don't act the way you want does not sound like making the relationship better. Maybe you should just leave.

This obviously didn't go the way Cheri had hoped. She failed to enlist Rho's cooperation and instead got resistance. She ended up being perceived as a threat and was rejected.

WHAT COULD HAVE BEEN DONE DIFFERENTLY

Timing: Cheri tried to bring up a cooperative topic while Rho was angry and frustrated. These emotions do not promote cooperative behavior. In an individual with symptoms of BPD, these emotions can encourage transient paranoid thinking. In the dialogue on pages 89–90, Rho ended up feeling threatened with abandonment—the worst nightmare of someone suffering symptoms of BPD.

While Cheri's effort to improve the relationship by setting a boundary might be successful with healthy individuals, her method made the communication with Rho unhealthier on three of four of our healthy connection directives. Setting boundaries with loved ones with BPD should be treated as a last resort, not a first option, as it undermines many of the healthy communications directives that we discussed earlier in this chapter.

Security: Cheri made Rho feel less secure by threatening to leave her. Had she offered affirmation and reassurance and then couched the communication in terms of trying to improve the relationship, she would have minimized the chance of getting a defensive response from Rho.

Stability: Cheri decreased the stability of the relationship by threatening to leave. She would have gotten a better response from Rho had she not threatened this.

Cooperation: Cheri failed to induce cooperation and increased competition by putting herself in a position to judge Rho's behavior and then punish (by leaving) bad behavior. Rho was not included in the process; the boundary was imposed on Rho. Cheri might have had a better outcome had she instead stated, "I would like us both to experience stability and security in our relationship now that we live together. I would like to talk with you about how we might accomplish this."

When attempting to enlist your loved one's cooperation in making healthy changes to the relationship, you must approach them in a way that does not make them feel criticized, blamed, or attacked. Once they have any of these reactions, they are likely to become less self-reflective and more defensive. Focusing on the following aspects of your approach will produce a better outcome.

Timing: Do not initiate a cooperative process during an argument. Individuals with symptoms of BPD are substantially emotion-driven, and the conflict will produce feelings of anger and frustration. You will do better to initiate the conversation during periods of affection or calmness.

Avoid threats: Individuals with symptoms of BPD respond very poorly to being threatened. They become defensive and sometimes combative.

Avoid criticism and blame: Individuals with symptoms of BPD respond defensively when approached this way. You can communicate the same information by making suggestions as to how each of you can contribute to a better relationship for both.

Enabling BPD Symptoms: Don't Feed the Monster

BPD is a monster of a disease. It can wreak havoc on relationships if allowed to. Even though you are not directly affected by the symptoms of this horrible disease, you need to make sure that your behavior doesn't make your loved one's BPD symptoms worse.

BPD symptoms affect the nervous system of your loved one in ways that cause them to lash out when frustrated. This causes instability in the relationship, which makes the relationship less secure and inhibits cooperation. It causes your loved one to seek codependent solutions as a way of reassuring themself that you will not abandon them. If you give in to these unhealthy processes, you will reinforce the BPD, enabling or feeding the monster.

If you refuse to reinforce these directives, then you starve the monster. You render processes such as lashing out and codependent manipulation ineffective, which forces your loved one to seek healthier alternatives.

The most important thing to remember when you are starving your loved one's monster is that you must be consistent. In practice, this means that you must not give in to your loved one's tantrums, testing, and guilting. If your loved one asks something of you respectfully, and you agree to do it, there is no problem. But if you say no to your loved one and they respond with anger or other hurtful behavior and you give in, you reinforce that hurting you is a good way for your loved one to get what they want.

Similarly, if your loved one asks you to do something that they should do for themself and you agree to it, you are encouraging codependency. Every time you give in, your efforts to starve the monster go back to zero. This is called variable reinforcement (of the monster/disease), which is the most powerful way to increase the undesirable behavior.

Starving your loved one's monster is respectful and loving. You should be overt and clear about how you cannot give in to their hurtful behaviors, because if you do, you are enabling their behavior to hurt the relationship. Then you can offer a healthier alternative that will address their needs and wants.

Note that your loved one might not accept that their behavior is hurting your relationship. Keep in mind that if your loved one is not at some point able to accept that their behavior, driven by an illness, is disrupting your relationship, you will not be able to significantly improve the situation.

FEED GABBY, NOT THE MONSTER

Jordan and Janelle adopted their daughter as an infant. As an infant, Gabby never seemed happy. She frequently cried and had tantrums. The new parents tried everything to comfort the child. Holding Gabby and swaddling her gave little relief and sometimes made her more agitated.

Jordan and Janelle felt like bad parents. They took Gabby to her pediatrician, who told them that there was nothing physically wrong with her but that the child needed more attention. He told them to be patient and indulgent.

This set the stage for Gabby's entire childhood. She became increasingly demanding. This made the parents feel more guilty and more useless. They continued to try to be more accommodating. As soon as Gabby started crying or yelling, they gave in to her every demand.

Gabby entered adolescence and ultimately adulthood without any skills for tolerating frustration. Her enabling parents taught her that being impatient and having tantrums will get her whatever she wanted. When Gabby left home to go to college, she found that crying and having tantrums did not work outside the home. She was unable to cope, so she dropped out of college and came home.

Though well-meaning, her parents and her doctor enabled her BPD symptoms by giving in to her. Her monster was well-fed. Gabby ended up without healthy coping mechanisms, and it left her unable to function successfully in society.

WHAT COULD HAVE BEEN DONE DIFFERENTLY

At some point, the parents needed to say no to Gabby and back it up. This would have forced her to develop healthy coping mechanisms to deal with her frustration.

Jordan and Janelle got overwhelmed by guilt and lack of experience in parenting. They should have sought support as adoptive parents of a troubled child. A developmental expert would have guided them as to how to not give in to Gabby while at the same time teaching her how to cope with frustration more successfully.

As a young adult, Gabby's expectations have crystallized. She has not had to take responsibility for herself before. It will be hard for her to understand why she has to now.

It is critical that her experience in college be a learning experience for her. She might be inclined to blame the school or the other kids at the school for her dysfunction. It is critical that her parents hold her responsible for her behaviors and choices that led to her needing to come home so that she can work on changing these behaviors and choices and pursue success.

Validating Gabby—by agreeing that she is a victim of the college and the student body—would feed her BPD monster and make her sicker, and therefore should be avoided.

Now that you understand the concept of enabling, or feeding the monster, take some time to reflect on how you might be enabling your loved one to be sick without realizing it. Note your enabling behaviors in your journal along with a plan to react in healthier ways.

In the previous example, the parents should note that they have enabled their daughter's illness by giving in to her tantrums and by not holding her responsible for her behavior and choices. They can use this information to make a plan to hold her to healthy expectations and develop mechanisms for coping with frustration.

TALK IT OUT

It is very important that your loved one understand that the changes you are making are designed to improve the relationship by neutralizing your previously enabling behaviors. If they don't, they will likely experience you as being withholding and perhaps abandoning them.

When discussing these changes with your loved one, you should characterize the changes as being targeted at minimizing unhealthy aspects of the relationship. You can introduce to them the four directives previously described (security, stability, independence, and cooperation). They are much more likely to embrace these changes if they can see the relationship as needing improvement rather than seeing themself as being defective and needing improvement.

Of course, their acknowledgment that they have something wrong with them is necessary for them to recover from symptoms of BPD, but this acceptance should be saved for the therapist's office while you focus on the relationship.

In this chapter, you learned how to steer the relationship with your loved one in a healthier direction. You probably also realized that you were enabling the unhealthy aspects of your relationship and your loved one's illness. This is a critical realization and will guide you in improving the relationship, but it is also a heavy burden for you.

Take some time to reflect on your enabling behaviors. Explore whether you might be doing this in other relationships as well. It will be very helpful for you to see the changes that you are making in the relationship as not just being for your loved one, but also for self-improvement. It will make you a better person and a better partner and therefore will feel like less of a burden or sacrifice.

Key Takeaways

- Communication with your loved one defines the connection that you have. Changes in the connection require changes in communication.

- Healthier relationships can be achieved by focusing on security, stability, independence, and cooperation.

- You might be enabling your loved one's illness.

- You can grow as a person while you steer the relationship toward a healthier connection.

6 Practicing Self-Care

Thus far, we have focused on how your loved one's symptoms of BPD affect the relationship. Now we are going to focus on keeping you well, because you can't function in a healthy relationship if you are not healthy.

This chapter will focus on how to take care of yourself as you endeavor to heal and grow the relationship with your loved one with symptoms of BPD. First, you will learn how to identify the emotions you experience in this relationship, and then you will learn tools for coping.

The first thing for you to keep in mind is that maintaining a relationship with a person with symptoms of BPD and trying to help them cope with their symptoms is a gargantuan undertaking. You must keep in mind your limitations: you cannot change the relationship on your own, and you cannot heal your loved one. You *can* minimize enabling and maximize support of healthy directions. Ultimately, the outcome of your efforts depends on your loved one's capabilities and willingness to cooperate. ●

Acknowledge Your Emotions

Having a close relationship with someone with symptoms of BPD can be a roller coaster. The instability that your loved one experiences internally causes emotional instability in all of their close relationships.

Your emotional experience with your loved one is a product of two factors: the event that stimulates the emotion and the way that you process the event and the emotion. Your emotions, like your vision and your hearing, are a sense. They are produced by your nervous system as a way of informing you about your environment and how you interact with it. Never ignore your feelings. That would be like riding your bicycle through city streets with your eyes closed.

Some emotions are uncomfortable. They inform you about aspects of your environment that you need to attend to. For example, if you feel cold, your nervous system is telling you that you are losing heat calories too quickly. If you ignore the cold, you will get colder. If you continue to ignore it, you will get frostbite or hypothermia.

This section presents emotions that are commonly experienced when your loved one has symptoms of BPD, along with coping strategies for how to deal with them. You need to acknowledge these feelings and cope, or you will probably eventually get sick.

ANGER

Anger is caused by pain. If someone or something is hurting you or might hurt you, you will get angry. The expression of anger, such as by yelling, threatening, or being aggressive, pushes away the perceived source of the pain. If you want to stop being angry, you must address the source of your pain.

If your relationship with your loved one is the source of your pain, it challenges the relationship. Your first step should be to talk to your loved one and try to get them to cooperate in changing their behavior so that they are not hurting you anymore. This is the best solution, because if they cooperate not only will your pain go away, but their healthy cooperation will actually make you feel closer to them.

If your loved one does not cooperate, the next step is to set boundaries. If your loved one respects your boundaries, or if you are successfully able to maintain them, it will reduce your pain, but this will not make you feel closer to them.

For example, if you ask your loved one not to bring up a topic that is painful for you and they cooperate, you will feel closer to them. If they don't cooperate, you will have to set a boundary by stopping them when they do bring it up. If they refuse to stop talking about it, you will feel resentment, which will cause you to feel less close to them. You also will not be able to trust them, because they are demonstrating that your best interest is not a priority to them.

If the first two steps don't relieve your pain, then you will have to make a choice: either accept that you will be in pain as a price to pay for being in the relationship, or end the relationship to relieve the pain.

FRUSTRATION

Frustration is what you feel when you don't get what you want. If your loved one prevents you in some way from pursuing goals that are meaningful to you, they will be a source of frustration to you. The experience of frustration generally makes us want to remove the source. If your loved one becomes a source of frustration, you will feel like not being around them as much, or at all.

The first step to coping with your frustration is to talk to your loved one and try to get cooperation. Intimate connections are made more intimate and more satisfying when they are fundamentally cooperative. The opposite of cooperation is competition, which makes relationships less intimate. A cooperative solution is always beneficial to intimate relationships.

Coping with frustration, or obstruction of progress toward your goal, involves changing either your strategy or your goal.

For example, Sam shared an apartment with their partner, Julie. After a recent robbery on the next block, Sam looked into ways that they and Julie could be safer in their building. Sam's goal was for Julie to work with them to make their living space safer.

When Sam asked Julie to work with them on increasing security, Julie stated that she felt secure and saw no reason to spend money on an alarm system. She declined to participate with Sam.

Sam purchased an alarm system, but Julie did not follow through on setting the alarm. Sam needed to change their method, by getting a passive alarm system that sets itself. This way, Sam would not need to depend on Julie to help keep them both safe. Or, Sam could have changed their goal. This might involve only keeping themselves safe, rather than them and Julie. They might, for example, take a class in self-defense.

FEAR

You feel fear when you feel threatened. This causes you to feel heightened or energized in preparation to flee the perceived threat. If your loved one threatens or frightens you, it will make you want to get away from them. Anything that causes you to feel like you want to get away from your loved one is destructive to the relationship.

Your first effort should be to get your loved one to cooperate in stopping the behavior that is threatening to you. If your loved one cooperates, you will feel closer to them.

If they don't, you have to go it alone. You might try to avoid situations where threatening behaviors occur. For example, if your loved one becomes aggressive when drunk, then you make sure that you are not around them when they are drinking.

Many people who have loved ones with symptoms of BPD are afraid of their loved one's anger and lashing out. In order to avoid being subject to the lashing out, they are guarded and withholding most of the time. This is sometimes described as "walking on eggshells." The guardedness prevents spontaneous expression of emotion and discourages closeness and intimacy.

If these partial-avoidance strategies don't work, then you will have to either tolerate the fear or end the relationship.

HOPELESSNESS

Hopelessness is generally the result of unresolved frustration. It is the state that people experience when they have tried everything they can think of but have not reached their goal. When your loved one has symptoms of BPD, you might experience hopelessness if you have not been able to get your loved one to cooperate with your efforts to improve the relationship.

While frustration is empowering in that it drives you to try harder, hopelessness is generally associated with helplessness, which is disempowering. It makes you want to give up. This feeling of giving up may be a sign of impending depression. This is an example of how your relationship can make you sick. You try your best to make the relationship better. You struggle with frustration associated with lack of cooperation from your loved one, and then you start to get depressed.

You must not let hopelessness disempower you. This is a signal that you will need to consider a broader spectrum of solutions. In the case of a romantic partner, this is when you need to seriously consider if the relationship is viable. You may have to either end the relationship or end the intimate aspects of the relationship. For familial relationships, you may have to create distance or set new boundaries with your loved one.

If you are not able to do this, you will need to seek help. Immobilization is a sign of depression, and you might need to be treated before you can effect necessary changes in your relationship.

GRIEF

If you are struggling with a difficult relationship with a loved one with symptoms of BPD, you may experience periods of grief. This feeling occurs when you experience a sense of loss, such as the loss of closeness with your loved one.

The sense of loss can come from a number of different areas:

- The instability that is characteristic of relationships affected by BPD symptoms, also known as the roller coaster, produces moments of intense closeness followed by abrupt withdrawal. This abrupt withdrawal of your loved one will produce grief.

- Being around stable relationships may make you feel like you are missing out on the opportunity to have stable relationships in your own life. In the case of romantic relationships, you may be grieving the lost opportunity to have a better relationship by staying in the current one.

- Enabling BPD symptoms may cause you to feel grief from loss of self. Giving in to the lashing out of others or inhibiting your natural expression, such as walking on eggshells, causes you to forsake aspects of yourself to pacify the relationship.

If you have a family member or partner with symptoms of BPD and they do not cooperate with your efforts to make the relationship more stable and secure, then you have to take steps on your own to cope with grief. Seeking the stability and security that you cannot get from your relationship will require that you take time alone to fulfill and fortify yourself. We will discuss "me" time later in this chapter.

Seeking stability and security in other relationships may cause your loved one to feel threatened. They may express jealousy or envy, or they may interfere with your efforts to be close to others.

If you have moved from frustration to hopelessness and now to grief and you still have not made sufficient changes to your life, this means that if you continue in this direction, you are likely to become depressed, if you are not already sick. Professional help might be necessary.

SHAME

Shame comes from a sense of feeling damaged or defective. The self-loathing caused by BPD causes sufferers to avoid taking responsibility for errors, because this contributes to their feelings of self-loathing. Frequently being blamed for things that are not your fault may result in your feeling shame.

Individuals with symptoms of BPD often manifest impulsive and provocative behaviors in public. If you are with them, you might experience shame by association. For example, Carrie was mortified every time her friend yelled at people for not picking up after their dogs in the public park.

This will cause you even more shame if these provocative behaviors are targeted toward you. For example, Rex was very attracted to his boyfriend, Ray, but he felt very uncomfortable when Ray kissed him in front of his coworkers.

If your experience of shame is limited to reactions to your loved one's behavior, you should try to get your loved one to cooperate by modifying their behavior. If they don't cooperate, you might try to avoid situations with your loved one where you might feel shamed by their behavior. For example, Rex can avoid having Ray around his work friends.

Feeling responsible for the decisions or behaviors of others is a form of boundary violation. Healthy boundaries require individuals to take responsibility for their choices and behaviors and not those of others. When Carrie's friend is yelling at the dog owner in the park, Carrie can take a step back and look away, signaling that she is not part of that behavior and does not take responsibility for it.

If you experience shame in numerous situations in your life, the healthiest solution is personal growth. This begins with rigorous self-reflection. Take an inventory of yourself and identify what aspects you are ashamed of. Those that you can change or improve upon, you should. Those that you cannot, you should learn to be proud of, or at least accept.

SELF-BETRAYAL

Individuals with loved ones with BPD sometimes feel like they are betraying themselves by staying in the relationship. They often feel exploited by giving in to persistent demands for reassurance and affirmation. They feel foolish for complying with these demands, but do so to avoid conflict.

Loved ones of sufferers of BPD symptoms also frequently feel demeaned. This comes from being asked to do simple tasks that their loved ones should be doing for themselves as well as from being criticized or attacked during periods of lashing-out behavior.

Allowing yourself to be exploited and/or demeaned is likely to cause feelings of self-betrayal. You are allowing yourself to be treated this way. You feel like you are betraying yourself, because you are.

If you cannot get cooperation from your loved one in adjusting the relationship so that you don't feel this way, then you will have to change your behavior. You cannot allow yourself to engage in behaviors that make you feel like you are betraying yourself. If you don't address this, it will undermine your confidence in yourself, increase your anxiety, and feed the monster that is hurting your loved one.

This does not mean that you can never do things for your loved one or make compromises. You probably wouldn't mind calling your mother more often when she is lonely or sick, but if you had to call her twice per day every day, you would probably feel exploited and overly burdened.

Allowing others to demean you or act hurtfully in any way is unhealthy. You should always do whatever is necessary to stop others from mistreating you.

A common feature of individuals with symptoms of BPD is weak empathy. So if you want your loved one to know how you feel, you will have to tell them. But first, you should be clear with yourself why you want your loved one to know how you feel.

Most people share their feelings with loved ones for the purpose of having them address the feelings in some way, often in the hope that they will be validated. If you are expressing feelings that don't relate to your relationship with your loved one, they will probably be able to validate those feelings. For example, if you are frustrated with your boss and share this with your loved one, they will probably be able to understand why you are annoyed.

You will have a harder time getting your loved one to validate feelings that you have in reaction to their own behavior. When you express feeling anger, frustration, or shame as a result of their behavior they are likely to feel blamed and attacked. This will increase their self-loathing, and they might lash out at you.

The following suggestions will maximize the chance that your loved one will cooperate in making the relationship better and minimize the chance that they will lash out:

- **Timing:** Bring up these conversations during tranquil periods, not in the middle of an argument. Conflict makes your loved one less receptive to hearing your feelings and cooperating.

- **Context:** Begin the conversation with reassurance and affirmation of your love and your desire to have a better relationship.

- **Present your feelings in a cause-and-effect format.** Explain what makes you feel frustrated, angry, etc. without being accusatory. For example, do not phrase it as "You make me feel frustrated." Instead say, "It makes me feel frustrated when people tell me what to do."

- **Ask for specific changes in behavior; do not demand them.** Let them know that their cooperation is appreciated, not taken for granted.

- **If possible, give examples** of occasions where your loved one already uses the desired behaviors with you.

Seek Support

Dealing with a loved one with symptoms of BPD can be very isolating. Many individuals with symptoms of BPD are able to be charming in casual settings. People who don't know them intimately may have never seen their insta-bility or lashing out. This may leave you alone with your feelings. Reaching out to others can be very helpful, but it is important that you are selective in choosing who you reach out to and how you do it.

FAMILY AND FRIENDS

You will naturally want to reach out to family and friends if you are in distress related to your relationship with a loved one with symptoms of BPD. A significant hazard associated with reaching out to family and friends is that you might create triangulation. This occurs when a rela-tionship of three is perceived as two against one. The risk of triangulation is high in this circumstance as individuals with symptoms of BPD often experience transient paranoia. This makes them particularly suspicious of loved ones doing things behind their back. They are likely to see this as a betrayal.

You also should keep in mind that if you complain about your loved one to your friends or relatives and then later resolve your issues with your loved one, your friends and relatives will still be aware of all the negative information you shared with them about your loved one. For this reason, consider seeking other forms of support. However, if you do reach out to your friends and relatives for support, here are some tips.

TALK ABOUT IT

Before you approach your friend or relative to discuss your difficulties with your loved one with BPD symptoms, you should ask yourself what you hope to gain in opening up to them. Looking for sympathy encourages triangulation because it makes you the victim and your loved one the villain.

Your best option is to seek from your friend or relative the sense that you are not alone. When pursuing this goal, your focus should be on what you feel and what you are going through rather than your loved one's behaviors.

You should not approach a friend or relative and:

- "Vent" to them

- Focus on complaining about your loved one

- Present yourself as a victim

- Diagnose your loved one

- Ask them to intervene in the relationship

You should discuss:

- Your feelings (e.g., isolation, alienation, loneliness, frustration, etc.)

- Your needs

- Any topic that might give you a break from thinking about your relationship

THERAPY

Seeking help and support from a professional is your best choice. Several different types of therapy can be helpful to you depending on your circumstances. Specific resources are listed at the end of this book (page 147).

- **Medical:** If you have developed physical or psychiatric symptoms related to your experience with someone with BPD, you should seek appropriate medical care. This includes stress-related symptoms such as severe anxiety, panic, depressed mood, headaches, stomachaches, chest pain, etc.

- **Supportive psychotherapy:** A supportive psychotherapist will help you sort out your feelings and make choices that are best for you. This type of therapy will be most helpful if the therapist has training and experience working with people with personality disorders.

- **Behavior therapy:** Dialectical behavior therapy (DBT) was designed for BPD. Learning the techniques of DBT and working with a therapist experienced in the use of these techniques will provide helpful guidance as you seek to improve or change the relationship.

- **Insight-oriented therapy:** This will help you more in the longer term to understand why you choose to engage in a relationship that is difficult and sometimes hurtful.

SUPPORT GROUPS

In-person support groups can be very helpful. You will have the opportunity to share experiences with others going through similar challenges in their lives and families. Check with your local hospitals and mental health clinics for availability. You can also seek referrals from your local or state psychological association.

ONLINE COMMUNITIES

Online communities have become much more popular since the advent of COVID-19. They offer a larger community but may not have as consistent a population. Two sources of support groups specifically for individuals and families affected by BPD are PDAN (Personality Disorder Awareness Network) and StopWalkingOnEggshells.com. These two groups run online support groups as well as offer courses, podcasts, etc.

Find Some "Me" Time

Individuals with symptoms of BPD often use emotional projection. When they are frustrated, they communicate this to you by making you feel frustrated. They do this by interrupting your suggestions or by rejecting them out of hand. You will quickly feel just like them: frustrated. In addition, these individuals tend to be needy, which makes them demanding of your time, attention, and other resources.

When feeling exhausted, frustrated, exploited, etc. by your relationship, you need to take a break and find some "me" time. Take this time to regroup or reset yourself. Seek activities that you generally find rejuvenating. Exercise, hiking, meditation, yoga, napping, reading, etc. are all fine choices.

As you begin to feel rejuvenated, you should take some time to reflect on your situation. The frequent blame and projection can leave you feeling guilty, inadequate, or selfish. Take this solitary time to look at yourself objectively. Ask yourself: Are you really selfish or are they just saying that to get what they want? Do others in your life accuse you of being selfish?

Having restored your sense of self, you should reflect on the relationship. What are the long-term costs to you of being in this relationship? What is a realistic expectation of what can change in the relationship? You must not stay in a relationship that makes you sick. A person who loves you will not want you to be sick.

HOW YOUR LOVED ONE MIGHT FEEL

Many individuals with symptoms of BPD experience significant fear of abandonment and transient paranoia. They are likely to experience your choosing to be alone as either a rejection or put-down, or both. Due to their own fears of being alone, they do not easily understand why you would choose to be alone rather than being with them for any reason.

They experience your alone time as your punishing them, and it makes them feel victimized by you. They may lash out at you or threaten to abandon you or punish you in some other way.

You can minimize the pain your loved one feels when you take "me" time by how you present it to them. Even with the best presentation, many people with symptoms of BPD are sensitive to intimate attachments withdrawing from them, so you should be prepared for the possibility that their response will be noncooperative. Handling such reactions is discussed in the next chapter.

WRITE IT DOWN

Use your journal to track the changes in your body and sense of well-being on a scale from 1 to 10 where 1 is very mild and 10 is unbearable. Take a few pages in your journal and make columns under each emotional or body disturbance and then update this chart each week. This allows you to track trends that signal deterioration of your health, possibly attributable to the relationship. Failure to act on these trends can produce catastrophic results for your health, such as heart attack, stroke, etc., as well as insidious health events, such as deterioration of your immune system, ability to focus, etc., that become catastrophic if not addressed. Note not only the direction of changes from week to week (better or worse), but also the slope or steepness of the change. If your health is deteriorating quickly, take action immediately. Chapter 7 will focus on what steps you might need to take next.

TAKE A MINDFUL MINUTE

In this chapter, you learned that your relationship can make you sick if you let it. Some types of illness come upon you suddenly, like a heart attack or stroke, which can be made worse by stress. Other types of disorders or digestive issues, such as ulcers, depression, anxiety disorders, etc., can creep up on you. Because they emerge slowly, you might not be aware of them until substantial damage is done.

Take a moment to assess the cost on your body and sense of well-being that you pay to be in this relationship. Spend a few minutes checking in with your body and note aspects of your functioning that are suboptimal or getting worse. For example, have you been having headaches or digestive issues that you have not had before? Are you having trouble sleeping or concentrating? Have you lost your patience? It's important to track any damage to your body or mental state to prevent becoming vulnerable to serious illness in the future.

Key Takeaways

- An unhealthy relationship can make you physically and emotionally sick.

- Self-care requires self-monitoring of your emotions and overall health.

- Having "me" time is very important to your mental health, especially when you are in a difficult relationship.

- Help is out there for you in the form of professionals and support groups.

7 Staying Safe

A healthy relationship requires two healthy
people. This chapter will focus on keeping yourself and your loved one safe. There are different
levels of safety in close relationships. The base
level is physical safety. Emotional safety refers
to protecting yourself from hurtful behaviors
that are designed to make you feel bad. A third
level of safety concerns the durability of the
relationship: its ability to withstand conflict and
disagreement. This is often referred to as security, reliability, or dependability.

Feeling unsafe is one of the primary drivers of
anxiety. The more unsafe you feel, the more anxious you will feel. A panic attack is an intolerable
level of fear. If you are walking on eggshells in an
intimate relationship, you are anxious most or all
of the time. If you fail to address high levels of
persistent anxiety, you will probably get sick. ●

Set Behavior Boundaries

Unsafe behavior in intimate relationships is destructive to both individuals and the relationship itself. If you can get cooperation from your loved one and the two of you can stop it together, this will increase your intimacy and benefit the relationship. If not, then you will have to set boundaries.

The weak empathy often associated with symptoms of BPD can cause boundary violations, so the importance of setting safety-related boundaries cannot be overemphasized. Safety can be compromised by a lack of boundaries in any of the following three ways:

- BPD sometimes causes sufferers to violate the **physical safety** of others. This can occur impulsively, such as by lashing out physically in a tantrum or engaging in promiscuous behaviors.

- **Emotional safety** in an intimate relationship is threatened when one or both parties say or do things that hurt the feelings of the other.

- **Relationship safety** is compromised in intimate relationships by making threats to break up with your partner or by being unfaithful.

If you do not set boundaries where needed, you are letting your loved one hurt you. This is bad for your loved one, because it feeds their monster. It rewards them for unhealthy behaviors, thus increasing the frequency and intensity of those behaviors. It is bad for you, because allowing others to hurt you decreases your self-worth and self-esteem. And it is bad for the relationship, because naturally you will want to push someone away who's hurting you, which decreases closeness and intimacy.

Boundaries should be expressed in clear and simple terms. The first time you state your boundaries, you do not need to state consequences; otherwise, your loved one is likely to hear it as an ultimatum or a threat.

When setting boundaries with loved ones, start with the least possible amount of aggression and then raise the level as needed. The progression is:

1. Statement of boundary

2. Statement of boundary with consequences

3. Enforcement of boundary using consequences stated in step 2

Here are some examples of boundary-setting statements:

"Never raise your hand to me again."

"When I say no, you have to stop what you are doing to me."

"Next time you borrow my car, you need to ask me first."

"It hurts my feelings when you look at your cell phone while we are talking."

Hopefully, these expressions will get a cooperative response showing a willingness to honor the boundary stated. If your loved one responds noncooperatively, such as by arguing or refusing to honor your request, then you will need to restate the boundary with a consequence. Here are some examples:

"If you raise a hand to me again, I will call the police."

"If you do not respect my saying no, I will not be alone with you again."

"If you don't stop taking my car without asking me, I will have to hide my keys."

"Put down your cell phone, or this conversation is over."

CARL PAYS FOR FEEDING THE MONSTER

Carl was a divorced parent with a twenty-four-year-old daughter, Shannon. He always thought of her as Daddy's little girl and took pleasure in spoiling her. She was his only child, and he gave her whatever she wanted.

Shannon lived in an apartment that Carl paid for. She did some freelance writing when she could, but she didn't work many hours, because Carl had supplied her with a credit card for all of her expenses.

Carl had to tell his daughter that he had fallen in love and was going to get married, so he took her out to a restaurant for dinner. He hoped that she would be joyful for him and be a part of his new family constellation, but he was also concerned about her jealousy. She had refused to acknowledge any of his other friends and lovers.

CARL: I have someone I would like you to meet.

SHANNON: Not that again.

CARL: What again?

SHANNON: You want me to meet one of your lovers.

CARL: This is very special.

SHANNON: They are all special.

CARL: I am going to get married.

At this point, Shannon stood up and poured a glass of water over Carl's head. He was shocked, but he also had considered the possibility that Shannon would have a bad reaction. He should have set a safety boundary with her at that time. He might have said, "I am interested in how you feel, but you may not be physically aggressive with me."

Instead, he begged her to sit back down, which she did. He didn't even mention the physical attack. He resumed the conversation.

> **CARL:** Shannon, I have the right to move on with my life.

> **SHANNON:** It's always about you. You are a poor excuse for a father.

Now Carl was being emotionally abused. This was another opportunity to set a boundary. He could have said, "Stop saying hurtful things to me so that we can go on with this conversation." He ignored the verbal/emotional abuse and tried to continue the conversation.

> **CARL:** Why are you giving me such a hard time?

At this, Shannon stood up, turned over her plate of food, and walked out of the restaurant. Carl's failure to set safety-related boundaries resulted in an increase in conflict and hurtful behaviors. He fed her BPD monster and reinforced that throwing things at him and insulting him in public is not only tolerated, but effective in ending the conversation about her meeting her father's spouse-to-be.

Carl would have had a better outcome if he had installed the boundaries previously suggested. If Shannon refuses to cooperate with Carl's boundaries, he will have to come up with a consequence. He might have stated something like this:

"Shannon, I am trying to move on with my life and include you in a way that honors you and makes us closer. I want to discuss this with you and come to a solution that works for both of us. Your hurtful behavior will only make this problem worse. If you cannot cooperate with me, then I will be less cooperative with you. You are twenty-four years old, and I am not obligated to support you if you do not cooperate with me in some basic ways."

If Behaviors Spin Out of Control

A number of individuals experience severe symptoms of BPD. These individuals suffer the most discomfort and dysfunction. Naturally, the impact of the symptoms on intimate relationships is worse in more severe cases. The following BPD-related behaviors can create hazardous circumstances to you and your loved one and must not be ignored. They all require immediate and firm responses. This section focuses on how to manage the most severe expressions of the disorder and offers guidance on responding to these behaviors if they arise in your relationship.

PHYSICAL

Individuals with severe symptoms of BPD may engage in behaviors that are hurtful and dangerous to both of you. These behaviors may include physical assault, self-mutilation, and destruction of property. Examples of physical assault include punching, kicking, spitting on others, throwing things at others, etc. Self-mutilation can include cutting or burning themselves, pulling out hair, biting nails, etc. Destruction of property includes damage and defacement of vehicles, homes, artwork, etc.

Physical acting out must not be tolerated. If physical acting out is at all successful in getting your loved one what they want, it will lead to more frequent and more intense physical acting out. Eventually, someone will probably get hurt.

Use of the form-before-content tool is suggested here. Upon the first sign of physical acting out—a shove, hitting a wall, being rough with a pet, for example—everything stops and your loved one must be confronted. Use the following steps in order.

1. State the boundary. For example, "Don't ever push me again."

2. If they continue, ask them directly whether or not they are in control of themself. If they reply that they cannot control themself, then you must take steps to control them. Calling 911 may be a final resort.

3. If they respond that they are in control, tell them what will happen if they don't stop immediately. For example, "If you touch me one more time, I will walk out and never come back."

EMOTIONAL

Individuals suffering from symptoms of BPD often experience emotional dysregulation, causing them to be emotionally hurtful. This most often occurs with those they are closest to because the dysregulation is triggered by frustration and they experience more frustration in relationships that they rely on.

The purpose of emotional acting out is generally either to get you to do something for them, to stop you from doing something they don't want you to do, or to call attention to themselves. Here are some examples of emotional acting out that are often seen in individuals with BPD:

- **Verbal abuse.** This involves deprecating statements about you and often includes profanities,
  name-calling, and screaming.

- **Indictments.** This involves making hurtful statements
  about your character, ability, or intent. Examples
  include "You are the worst father," "You stink in bed,"
  "You hate me," etc.

- **Triangulation.** This is when your loved one enlists
  the sympathy of another in order to gang up on
  you. This can be very destructive to families when a
  sibling triangulates a parent against the other sibling, or a parent triangulates their child against the
  other parent.

- **Shaming.** This is revealing private information
  about you to a third party for the purpose of
  embarrassing you.

- **Blaming.** This involves blaming you for things that
  are not your fault. This can include blame-shifting,
  where they blame you for something they did. It can
  also involve blaming you for things that are nobody's
  fault, like the weather spoiling a picnic.

- **Guilting.** This is when your loved one tries to make
  you feel guilty for not acquiescing to their demand
  or by calling you "ungrateful" after all they have done
  for you.

When your loved one is acting out emotionally, you
should take great care *not* to mirror them. Mirroring
hurtful behavior, such as raising your voice when being
yelled at, will escalate the hurtful behavior and make the
situation worse.

When approaching an emotionally dysregulated individual, you should move slowly and speak softly. You should

establish and maintain eye contact. You should use the form-before-content tool, where you only discuss the form until they stop being hurtful. In a soft voice you should say things to them such as "We can discuss what just happened once you calm down" or "This matter is between you and me. I will not discuss this in front of Mom."

Use as few words as possible and be prepared to stop talking if they escalate further. Stick with form-before-content, and they will eventually calm down. Once they do, you set necessary boundaries and then address the content. Remember, this is a process, not a single event. It might take more than one transaction before the form is acceptable. Be patient, but firm and consistent.

IMPULSIVITY

Impulsive behaviors often associated with symptoms of BPD include sexual promiscuity, gambling, overspending, and impulsive verbal behaviors, such as blurting out inappropriate comments or expressions.

The key to dealing with your loved one's impulsive behavior is holding them responsible for their actions. Don't clean up their messes or smooth things over for them. If they have spent too much money, they will have to either return what they bought or do without something until they pay for their indiscretion. If they say something inappropriate in public, they must either apologize or accept that they might no longer be welcome in certain settings. If they are sexually promiscuous, they will have to get tested for sexually transmitted infections (STIs) if they are going to be physically intimate with you.

DISTORTED PERCEPTION OF REALITY

When individuals with symptoms of BPD experience high levels of stress, their perception of reality may become distorted. The most common distortions are dissociation and paranoia.

Individuals experiencing significant dissociation should not be left alone. People in these states are partially or completely out of touch with their environment. This puts them at increased risk for dangerous behavior. If you cannot be with them until the dissociation resolves, you should make sure that they are with someone who can keep them safe.

During paranoid states, individuals with symptoms of BPD believe that others, including you, are out to hurt them. In moderate to severe cases, the suspicious thinking can be delusional. These are false beliefs that you are somehow deceiving or betraying them. They may accuse you of these offenses with no tangible evidence and then punish you, even though you are innocent. For example, Shira refused to sleep with her lover after accusing them of being with her best friend behind her back. When the lover provided an alibi, Shira just shook it off and said it was a lie.

Defending yourself or arguing with someone who is in a paranoid state will only make them more agitated. If you are the target of a paranoid delusion, it is helpful to validate their feelings, but not the delusional material. They are feeling threatened, frightened, angry, rejected, etc. You can validate these feelings, but do not validate that you did something you did not do. This makes the delusion worse and now you are lying to them. In the previous example, Shira's lover might have said this to her:

"Shira, I know that you care very much about me and that the thought of me being with someone else upsets you. That is understandable. I just want you to know that I care about you as well and will always do my best not to hurt you."

If your loved one asks directly whether or not you betrayed them, you must stick with the truth.

WRITE IT DOWN

When articulating safety-related boundaries to your loved one, it is important that you speak in clear and simple terms. It will help you to write in your journal the behaviors that need to change, your feelings about these behaviors, and the consequences of your loved one not complying. For example, the behavior that needs to change is unwanted touching. You feel violated. The consequence is that you will no longer see this individual in person, which removes their opportunity to violate your boundary.

Remember, you don't necessarily need to give all of this information to your loved one at once. You should start with telling them that they need to stop. If they persist, then you tell them the consequences. Whether or not you share your feelings depends on whether you think they are receptive and can respond compassionately. Noting your feelings in your journal will assist you in monitoring your health, which we discussed in the last chapter, and in monitoring the relationship, which will be discussed in the next chapter.

Maintaining an intimate relationship with an individual suffering from symptoms of BPD requires significant effort on your part and specialized skills. Needing to set and maintain boundaries may make you feel like you are doing more than your share of the work to sustain the relationship. These feelings are valid. You need to decide that the relationship with your loved one is special and gratifying enough that you are glad to do whatever it takes to make it work. Or you need to change the relationship and possibly end it. If you feel exploited or resentful, you will not be able to enjoy the relationship and you might make yourself sick with stress. Take some time to reflect on the value of the relationship and if you see your burden as worth it. This is the only path toward contentment.

Key Takeaways

- Tolerating an unsafe relationship can make you hurt or sick.

- Safety issues need to be a priority.

- Getting your loved one to cooperate is always the best solution.

- Without cooperation, you must resort to setting and enforcing boundaries.

8 Keeping Track of Your Relationship

Living with an insecure intimate attachment causes varying levels of stress and associated discomfort. This is particularly true if your primary attachment suffers from symptoms of BPD. The stress and other discomfort that you feel often causes frequent thoughts about whether or not you can or wish to continue in the relationship.

In this chapter, you will learn how to think about the insecurity and associated instability that you experience and how to make choices that are best for you. ●

Taking Stock

Healthy and secure relationships are associated with a persistent satisfaction from the stability of the relationship and the personal conviction that your relationship with your loved one is the best you can have. When your loved one has symptoms of BPD, you rarely experience this level of satisfaction. The instability causes you stress that can threaten your physical and mental health if you allow conditions to persist.

Taking stock of your relationship requires an overview of the relationship. You need to see patterns and trends of behaviors so that you don't overreact to single events. For this reason, you should take stock of the relationship during periods of calm, not during conflicts or right after your loved one hurts or annoys you.

Taking stock of a relationship is *not* an objective exercise. It is subjective and personal to you. Different individuals are troubled by different things. Your experiences, preferences, sensitivities, and ways of seeing the world matter, because you are the one that has to live with the relationship.

For example, Todd enjoyed spending time with his new girlfriend, Nina, who has symptoms of BPD. Like many individuals with BPD, she became jealous and suspicious about him paying attention to his friends and relatives, so she discouraged these relationships. She avoided getting together with his friends and relatives, and whenever Todd did see them, she would grill him about who was with and what they were doing. This made Todd extremely uncomfortable. Todd had the following conversation with his friend Drew, who had a different reaction:

DREW: When am I going to meet your new girlfriend, Nina?

TODD: I am not sure.

DREW: How about I take you guys out to dinner?

TODD: I asked her several times to meet my friends, but she likes to be alone with me.

DREW: Oh. Honeymoon syndrome.

TODD: No. She is jealous of my paying attention to others.

DREW: I am sure she will get over it after the two of you are together for a while.

TODD: As we get closer to each other, she seems to get more possessive.

DREW: Wow. I guess she really digs you.

TODD: I think it is just jealousy, and I am not sure it will ever go away.

DREW: Don't worry, she will get bored with being alone with you and welcome the chance to socialize with you in groups.

This conversation added to Todd's self-doubt, and he became more anxious. He began to wonder if maybe he was too sensitive and perhaps he should feel good about Nina wanting to be with him so much. The issue is not how Drew or anyone else might feel, but rather how Todd feels. This is where Todd needs to take stock of the relationship. This requires stepping back and imagining how he might feel if isolating behavior became the norm.

If you find yourself in a situation like Todd's, where you doubt your ability to be satisfied with your relationship, you will benefit from spending some time in your calm place or your happy place and asking yourself a series of questions that will help you evaluate your circumstances and choose your best options. Here are some suggestions.

- What hurts/irritates me the most about the relationship?

- How often does this occur?

- Is what I am feeling coming just from the relationship or are other situations in my life adding to what I am feeling?

- Am I encouraging the relationship or making it worse without realizing it?

- Is it getting better, worse, or staying the same over time?

- What can I do to make the situation better?

- Is my loved one capable of making changes for the better and willing to do so?

- Have I clearly communicated what is troublesome to me?

- Has it been understood?

- What are the positive aspects of the relationship?

- Does the good in the relationship outweigh the pain and discomfort?

- Can I maintain the relationship the way it is without getting sick?

Journaling your responses to these questions will help you get the bird's-eye view that you need to take stock. By making regular journal entries, you can track these patterns of behavior over time. This will help you determine how your efforts are affecting the relationship. For example, do you notice that the harder you try the worse things get? If so, your efforts might be undermining the relationship rather than supporting it. In the previous example, if Todd follows Drew's suggestion and becomes more tolerant of Nina's behavior, she may escalate and start to actively sabotage Todd's friendships. Noting this pattern in his journal will help Todd realize that he is actually feeding the monster and making Nina's illness worse. Seeing the pattern in his journal will help him respond appropriately.

When the Relationship Is Thriving

Intimate relationships with individuals who suffer from symptoms of BPD often have periods of intense closeness and excitement. This often occurs at the beginning of relationships, but these periods may occur intermittently throughout the relationship.

Many people whose loved ones have symptoms of BPD feel reluctant to do anything to disrupt the tranquility during these periods of closeness, but some things you can do to increase the stability of the relationship must be done during periods of relative calmness.

POSITIVE FEEDBACK

As a culture, we tend to focus more on complaints than compliments. In most situations, compliments are more effective. When you notice your loved one making efforts to improve or maintain the relationship, you should acknowledge it. For example, if Todd notices Nina asking a lot of questions about his friends or family members, he could say, "It's so nice to hear you're taking an interest in them. Should we make a plan to meet up with them? I'm sure they'll love you."

Noticing your loved one's efforts that are responsive to your expressions is particularly helpful. For example, if you have asked your loved one not to call you frequently for reassurance while you are traveling for business and then you notice that your loved one only called once during your last trip, you should say, "I noticed that you made an effort not to call me at work and that it might have been difficult for you. I really appreciate your effort."

ANTICIPATING SETBACKS

Individuals with symptoms of BPD often crave intimacy and seek it out. When they are successful in being intimate with another person, they often have difficulty regulating their attachment. They often become clingy or demanding, eventually resulting in their being disappointed by you. This is typically when the vulnerability to conflict and lashing out occurs.

While in the bliss of closeness, you might not want to think about the other phase of the pattern, but only by acknowledging the pattern can you prepare. Knowing that your loved one suffers emotional dysregulation and may become agitated after periods of calm gives you the opportunity to perceive the first signs of change in attitude. Here are a few adjustments that you can make under this circumstance to weather periods of dysregulation while minimizing the damage to the relationship.

- Offer reassurance and affirmation of your love and attachment to mitigate fear of abandonment.

- Inquire about your loved one's feeling state and offer to help.

- Understand your loved one's criticisms or other reactions as a combination of their internal distress and your behavior, and not just a reaction to your behavior.

These adjustments can help you and your loved one weather the instability with less pain and resentment. They may also shorten or decrease the intensity of difficult periods.

INTRODUCE NEW DIRECTIONS

Periods of closeness maximize the possibility that your loved one can hear suggestions for healing and growth constructively. You can introduce a conversation by saying something like "Wouldn't it be great if things were always this good between us?" You can follow this up by making suggestions like "Why don't we try meeting with a couple's counselor to help us keep things this way?"

When introducing new directions, try to present ideas in the positive light of relationship growth, and not in the negative light of criticism. Make sure you articulate your ideas as suggestions and not orders or demands.

If It's Time to End the Relationship

If you are seriously considering ending your relationship with a friend, relative, or partner, you must be in a lot of pain. Most likely, you are suffering internal conflict between your love for the person and the pain they cause you. There are generally three paths that will bring you to this point.

CATASTROPHIC EVENT

This is when your loved one does something that is so hurtful or offensive to you that you cannot live with it occurring even once. This could be a physical assault, infidelity, or anything that you find intolerable.

SLOW BUILDUP OF RESENTMENT AND ALIENATION

This occurs when non-catastrophic events occur with a frequency that have you feeling exhausted most of the time or when you need to put up so many boundaries that that there is little left to the relationship. It will help you to check with your journal to determine whether this is because you have been inconsistent in setting boundaries or whether your loved one refuses to accept the boundaries you have set. If you have been inconsistent, then you need to understand why. Is it because you are unable to maintain so many boundaries, or is it because you have not been enforcing them consistently? If you are incapable of setting and maintaining the boundaries necessary for your well-being, you must exit. If you have not been consistent enough, you need to understand why and either try harder or exit.

Relationships are in many ways defined by boundaries. If your loved one's behaviors are such that you need to install and maintain numerous boundaries consistently, you feel alienated from your loved one. This comes from having few, if any, activities that you can share with your loved one safely and securely.

YOU DEVELOP FEELINGS FOR SOMEONE ELSE

Difficult periods in relationships increase the vulnerability to developing feelings for others because your primary intimate relationship is not consistently satisfying your needs. While you are feeling hurt or resentful toward your loved one, others may offer you support and affection.

You need to be very careful in this circumstance. If you are starved for affection, you may have difficulty telling the difference between true feelings for someone else and desperation driven by deprivation. This can lead you from the frying pan into the fire: from one dysfunctional attachment right into another.

This is also the worst way to end a relationship with someone you love or loved, as it will leave them feeling abandoned and betrayed. For this reason, it is strongly recommended that you do not act on your attraction to others until you resolve your relationship with your loved one with symptoms of BPD.

MAKING THE BREAK

Depending on the nature of the relationship, you can choose to end it altogether, or you can end parts of the relationship while maintaining other parts. If your loved one with BPD is your parent or your child, you cannot completely sever the relationship. You can stop living with them. You can stop supporting them. You can stop sharing your life with them. You can stop talking to them. But you cannot divorce a blood relative.

In romantic relationships, you can end the romantic or sexual aspect of the relationship while attempting to preserve a friendship. Preserving aspects of the relationship while ending core transactions can only be done with cooperation from your loved one. Their reaction to your pulling away will be painful for them, and they may need to shut you out altogether. If so, the partial-relationship option will not be available to you.

TAKE A MINDFUL MINUTE

Thinking about ending your relationship is scary, but it is also empowering. Without consideration of this possibility, you will feel trapped, helpless, and hopeless. It is your last option and will bring pain to both you and your loved one in the short term. Your decision should focus on the long-term consequences for you and your loved one if you continue to sustain an unhealthy relationship. You increase the likelihood of your getting sick with every day that you continue a relationship that is hurtful to you. You also feed your loved one's monster by allowing them to behave unhealthily in their relationship with you, and that makes your loved one sicker.

Reflect on the patterns of behavior in your relationship and your efforts to find a healthy cooperative solution. Review your progress on the four dimensions discussed in chapter 5 that help you replace unhealthy connections with healthy ones.

Take your time. Once you face the reality of the situation, you will eventually feel a sense of resolve. Your feelings matter. Let them guide you, but do not let them dominate you.

Regardless of whether you make a full or partial break from the relationship, you should be as gentle as possible. This will likely cause your loved one considerable pain as their greatest fear—abandonment—comes to fruition.

Avoid arguing over historical facts or how you came to your decision. You should validate their pain but don't justify your decision, even though you will likely be asked to explain your decision to leave. You should avoid blaming your loved one, because doing so will likely cause them more pain by increasing their self-loathing. It is better just to tell them "This relationship is not right for me." This is your decision, so you should take responsibility.

Ending the relationship with your loved one does not justify their lashing out at you or trying to punish you. Be prepared to protect yourself from retribution by having an exit. Do not break up while away on vacation with them, as you cannot leave if it becomes unsafe. Consider having this conversation in a public place, like a restaurant, to mitigate any violent reaction and to facilitate your quick departure if necessary.

Once you make your decision, do not linger with it. The longer you wait, the more anxious you will become. You should also prepare a support network for yourself. Let individuals that you are close to know what you are preparing to do so that they can be available to help you mourn the end of the relationship.

Final Takeaways

You probably picked up this book because you were having difficulties in an intimate relationship that you suspected was different from other relationships. You probably experienced pain and stress intermittently or consistently due to the instability of the relationship and the way you were being treated.

Now that you have read this book, you understand that you are in a relationship with someone who is affected by a disease that causes them significant dysfunction in their relationships. The dysfunction is most pronounced in intimate relationships.

You have also learned that this relationship can make both you and your loved one sick or sicker. You may be making the relationship and the illness worse by enabling unhealthy behaviors.

You now have a systematic approach to resolving your difficulties with your loved one who suffers from symptoms of BPD. Your goal is to increase the security, stability, independence/autonomy, and cooperativeness. You have many tools you can use to effect this transition.

Attempting to get cooperation from your loved one should always be the starting point in making these changes. If you cannot garner their cooperation, you will have to use boundaries and other methods that do not require their willing cooperation. If this does not produce satisfactory results, you will have to end the relationship. If you do not, you will continue to feed the monster, and you and your loved one will get sicker.

The best chance for a beneficial outcome is a consistent effort to improve the relationship until all possibilities are exhausted. Knowing that everything that can be done was done brings resolve if you must leave. It also brings peace of mind knowing that you did your best and that no stone was unturned.

If your relationship improves as a result of your efforts, you will be closer to your loved one, and hopefully you can rally together toward healing and growth for both of you and for the relationship. If you have to end the relationship, you should prepare to mourn. Spend time reviewing the events of the relationship. Try to understand why you chose to be in a relationship with someone who has a significant mental illness and what might have attracted you to them.

You must pursue personal healing and growth throughout your life in order to be a healthy person and experience satisfaction. If others refuse to heal and grow, then you must leave them behind. You can bring others along if they are also interested in healing and growth. This is a powerful platform for any relationship to thrive and can lead to lifelong satisfaction and happiness.

RESOURCES

Emergency Services

911 from anywhere in United States will connect you with emergency services. This phone number should only be called during situations that pose an imminent threat to you, your loved one, or anyone else.

The National Domestic Violence Hotline at 1-800-799-7233 provides services to victims of domestic violence and those at risk.

The National Suicide Prevention Lifeline is a U.S.–based suicide prevention network of over 160 crisis centers that provide 24/7 service via a toll-free hotline with the number 1-800-273-8255. It is available to anyone in suicidal crisis or emotional distress.

BPD Websites, Support Groups, and Organizations

National Educational Alliance for Borderline Personality Disorder (NEABPD)

BorderlinePersonalityDisorder.org

NEABPD runs Family Connections classes for parents and other family members of loved ones with BPD. Family Connections is a free, evidence-based, twelve-class course that meets in person for two hours and requires one to two hours of homework and/or practice weekly. It provides education, skills training, and support for people who are supporting a sufferer of BPD.

NEABPD also offers a virtual option for families living far from Family Connections meeting locations or for those who prefer to take the course online.

Family Connections is based on research funded by the National Institute of Mental Health. Surveys show that after completing the course, family members experience decreased feelings of depression, burden, and grief, and more feelings of empowerment.

Personality Disorder Awareness Network (PDAN)

PDAN is an organization that provides information and advocacy for individuals with BPD and their families and loved ones. Resources offered on the website include articles and books for children as well as social media contacts.

Psychology Today

Psychologytoday.com offers referrals to a panel of experts in all areas of psychotherapy. A collection of articles about BPD and related disorders can be found here: PsychologyToday.com/us/blog/my-side-the-couch

Stop Walking on Eggshells

StopWalkingonEggshells.com is a website developed and maintained by Randi Kreger for individuals and their families with BPD. It offers articles, books, and support groups for individuals affected by BPD.

Books about BPD

Lobel, Daniel S. *When Your Daughter Has BPD: Essential Skills to Help Families Manage Borderline Personality Disorder.* Oakland, CA: New Harbinger Publications, Inc., 2017.

_____. *When Your Mother Has Borderline Personality Disorder: A Guide for Adult Children.* Emeryville, CA: Rockridge Press, 2019.

Mason, Paul T., and Randi Kreger. *Stop Walking on Eggshells: Taking Your Life Back When Someone You Care about Has Borderline Personality Disorder.* 3rd ed. Oakland, CA: New Harbinger Publications, Inc., 2020.

Kreger, Randi, Christine Adamec, and Daniel S. Lobel. *Stop Walking on Eggshells for Parents: How to Help Your Child (of Any Age) with Borderline Personality Disorder without Losing Yourself.* Oakland, CA: New Harbinger Publications, Inc., 2021.

REFERENCES

Amad, Ali, Nicolas Ramoz, Pierre Thomas, Renaud Jardri, and Philip Gorwood. "Genetics of Borderline Personality Disorder: Systematic Review and Proposal of an Integrative Model." *Neuroscience Biobehavioral Review* 40 (March 2014): 6–19. DOI: 10.1016/j.neubiorev.2014.01.003.

American Psychiatric Association. *Diagnostic and Statistical Manual of Mental Disorders*. 5th ed. Arlington, VA: American Psychiatric Publishing, Inc., 2013.

Ibrahim, Jeyda, Nicola Cosgrave, and Matthew Woolgar. "Childhood Maltreatment and Its Link to Borderline Personality Disorder Features in Children: A Systematic Approach." *Clinical Child Psychiatry and Psychology* 23, no. 1 (January 2018): 57–76. DOI: 10.1177/1359104517712778.

Lieb, Klaus, Mary C. Zanarini, Christian Schmahl, Marsha M. Linehan, and Martin Bohus. "Borderline Personality Disorder." *Lancet* 364, no. 9432 (July 2004): 453–461. DOI: 10.1016/S0140-6736(04)16770-6.

Lis, Eric, Brian Greenfield, Melissa Henry, Jean Marc Guilé, Geoffrey Dougherty. "Neuroimaging and Genetics of Borderline Personality Disorder: A Review." *Journal of Psychiatry and Neuroscience* 32, no. 3 (May 2007): 162–173.

Lobel, Daniel S. *When Your Daughter Has BPD: Essential Skills to Help Families Manage Borderline Personality Disorder.* Oakland, CA: New Harbinger Publications, 2017.

Mercer, Deanna, Alan B. Douglass, and Paul S. Links. "Meta-Analyses of Mood Stabilizers, Antidepressants and Antipsychotics in the Treatment of Borderline Personality Disorder: Effectiveness for Depression and Anger Symptoms." *Journal of Personality Disorders* 23, no. 2 (April 2009): 156–174. DOI: 10.1521/pedi.2009 .23.2.156.

Soloff, Paul H., Judith A. Lis, Thomas Kelly, Jack Cornelius. and Richard Ulrich. "Self-Mutilation and Suicidal Behavior in Borderline Personality Disorder." *Journal of Personality Disorders* 8, no. 4 (1994): 257–267. DOI:10.1521/pedi .1994.8.4.257.

Stern, Adolph. "Borderline Group of Neuroses." *The Psychoanalytic Quarterly* 7 (1938): 467–489. DOI:10.1080/21674086.1938.11925367.

Witt, S. H., F. Streit, M., Jungkunz, et. al. "Genome-Wide Association Study of Borderline Personality Disorder Reveals Genetic Overlap and Bipolar Disorder, Major Depression and Schizophrenia." *Translational Psychiatry* 7, no. 6 (June 2017): e1155. DOI: 10.1038/tp.2017.115.

Zanarini, Mary C., Frances R. Frankenburg, John Hennen, D. Bradford Reich, and Kenneth R. Silk. "The McLean Study of Adult Development (MSAD): Overview and Implications of the First Six Years of Perspective Follow-up," *Journal of Personality Disorders* 19, no. 5 (October 2005): 505–523. DOI: 10.1521/pedi.2005.19.5.505.

INDEX

A
Abandonment, fear of, 3,
    42–43, 71
Anger, 8, 46–47, 55, 100–101

B
Behavioral contracts, 87–92
Biological factors, 10
Blaming, 126
Borderline personality
    disorder (BPD)
    behavior patterns, 27–29,
        47–48
    causes, 10–12
    defined, 2–3, 17
    diagnosing, 1
    living with, 14–15
    symptoms, 3–9, 12–13
    talking about, 30–31
Boundaries
    behavior, 120–124
    consequences for
        violating, 80, 129
    example, 76–79
    maintaining, 75–76, 130

selecting, 75
setting, 15, 28–30, 32, 59
BPD. *See* Borderline
    personality disorder
    (BPD)

C
Childhood trauma, 11, 12
Codependency, 78, 81–82
Cognitive behavioral therapy
    (CBT), 52
Communication
    conscious vs. unconscious,
        70, 72
    content, 67–68
    example, 70–72
    form, 67–68
    mindful, 68
    patterns, 73–74
Comorbidities, 2–3, 13, 17
Competition, 83
Confrontation, 74
Connection, 81–87, 97
Cooperation, 83, 86,
    91, 130

Acknowledgments

First and foremost, I would like to acknowledge my wife Diane, my children Zachary and John, and my daughter-in-law Nicole for their consistent support and assistance. My beautiful family has given me the inspiration to devote much of my professional life to helping others experience the love and satisfaction that my family provides me.

Thank you to all of you who seek knowledge, strength, and tools to fight BPD. You were the ones who taught me what I am now imparting to others who may be suffering pain similar to yours. This is your gift to them.

Next, I would like to acknowledge the staff of Callisto Media for their guidance and support in the preparation of this manuscript. Their ability to work with me made me feel like part of a team and enhanced the quality of product. I would particularly like to thank Katherine De Chant, the primary editor. I would also like to thank Matt Buonaguro, the acquisitions editor, for helping conceive of this project and making it happen.

About the Author

 **Daniel S. Lobel, PhD**, is a clinical psychologist in private practice in Katonah, New York. He has been in practice for over 30 years. He has published research in both clinical and forensic psychology journals, and he lectures around the United States to both clinical and forensic audiences. He also has authored chapters in several textbooks in this field.

More recently, he has been focusing on working with families that suffer from borderline personality disorder. In 2017, he released his first book, *When Your Daughter Has BPD: Essential Skills to Help Families Manage Borderline Personality Disorder*. In 2019, he released his second book, *When Your Mother Has Borderline Personality Disorder: A Guide for Adult Children*. His third book was coauthored with Randi Kreger and Christine Adamec: *Stop Walking on Eggshells for Parents*, released in 2021. He also writes a blog, *My Side of the Couch*, which is hosted by *Psychology Today* on their website.

DISCOVERING MY NICHE

FINDING FULFILLMENT AND MEANING IN THE PERSON GOD CREATED ME TO BE

GARY A. CHAPMAN

WESTBOW
PRESS®
A DIVISION OF THOMAS NELSON
& ZONDERVAN

Scripture taken from the Holy Bible, NEW INTERNATIONAL VERSION®. Copyright © 1973, 1978, 1984, 2011 by Biblica, Inc. All rights reserved worldwide. Used by permission. NEW INTERNATIONAL VERSION® and NIV® are registered trademarks of Biblica, Inc. Use of either trademark for the offering of goods or services requires the prior written consent of Biblica US, Inc.

This book is a work of non-fiction. Unless otherwise noted, the author and the publisher make no explicit guarantees as to the accuracy of the information contained in this book and in some cases, names of people and places have been altered to protect their privacy.

WestBow Press books may be ordered through booksellers or by contacting:

WestBow Press
A Division of Thomas Nelson & Zondervan
1663 Liberty Drive
Bloomington, IN 47403
www.westbowpress.com
1 (866) 928-1240

Because of the dynamic nature of the Internet, any web addresses or links contained in this book may have changed since publication and may no longer be valid. The views expressed in this work are solely those of the author and do not necessarily reflect the views of the publisher, and the publisher hereby disclaims any responsibility for them.

Any people depicted in stock imagery provided by Thinkstock are models, and such images are being used for illustrative purposes only. Certain stock imagery © Thinkstock.

ISBN: 978-1-5127-3689-2 (sc)
ISBN: 978-1-5127-3690-8 (hc)
ISBN: 978-1-5127-3688-5 (e)

Library of Congress Control Number: 2016905717

Print information available on the last page.

WestBow Press rev. date: 5/31/2016

CONTENTS

DEDICATION

This book is lovingly dedicated to my wife, Janie, who has patiently walked with me as I continue to discover my own NICHE. Her presence and encouragement has made the journey that much more fulfilling.

WHEN YOU COME TO A FORK IN THE ROAD

The title of Yogi Berra's autobiography captures a sliver of wisdom for living. Yogi counseled us simply: "when you come to a fork in the road, take it." Growing up on Italian Hill in Saint Louis, Yogi had approached a neighborhood street intersection many times. He had learned life's decision points demand wisdom and practical action.

With practical wisdom, Gary Chapman provides help for those of us who are committed to discerning and doing God's best in and with our lives. Use Gary's NICHE model. Begin now. Take finding and stewarding your NICHE in life seriously.

As you read the pages ahead, allow Gary's model (and Yogi's sayings) to guide your future steps:

- "If you don't know where you are going, you will wind up somewhere else," observed Yogi. Faith is a gift to be paid forward. It requires discipline and discernment. Gary's NICHE model gives you a trustworthy pathway for finding your next steps in life and ministry.
- "It's like déjà vu all over again," said Yogi. Some of us are slow learners. We repeat our stumbles. Gary's model provides multiple points for us to find our blind spots, see our patterns, and choose our best directions.

- "It gets late early out there," Yogi once thought during a road trip. While it's never too late to hear God's calling in your ears, early starts and timely discoveries leave more years and additional opportunities for you to follow your calling. Start your NICHE pilgrimage now.
- "The game isn't over until it's over," claimed Yogi hopefully. God graces us with new beginnings. As long as you live and breathe, you can identify your NICHE and use it for holy ministry.

Your future lies in your hands and in God's heart. Read Gary's instructions now. Reflect now. Discover now. Act now. Your NICHE is your launch pad for new horizons.

Dr. Robert D. Dale
Writer–Coach–Teacher
Richmond, VA

PREFACE

"Who is your toughest leadership challenge? Yourself."
— Bill Hybels, pastor of Willow
Creek Community Church

In his book, *A Work of Heart*, author and leadership consultant Reggie McNeal wisely recognizes, "Self–understanding is the most important information you will need as a leader. And, that self–understanding begins and ends with God." Though a dimension of leadership often neglected by leaders, self–leadership provides clues as to who God created us to be, our values and convictions, what we're capable of doing, and why we do what we do.

There are a lot of people and agendas competing for our time, energy, commitment, money, etc. I know; I live in that world, too! Too easily we begin to compare ourselves and our life to that of others. To choose to model our life after others is not an altogether bad thing. But, if taken too far, we can shortchange ourselves, attempting to become someone we were never meant to be and spending our life engaged in tasks we were never meant to do.

That each of us is here in this specific period of human history is no coincidence. God placed us here for more than just a comfortable existence. In creating us, he has a specific purpose and influence in mind. At the same time, we're given the awesome privilege of charting our life's path with God.

My own personal experience and interactions with others, though, suggests discerning who we were created to be and our God–ordained purpose is easier said than done. Some simply opt to sleepwalk through life with no real purpose or meaning. Still others, allow the world and the agenda of others to map the course of their life. The truly wise, though, will do the hard work of getting to know the "real" person God created them to be. They soon discover that taking care of the "being" (who God created them to be) allows the "doing" (their God–given purpose in life) to more naturally follow.

A desire to become the best "self" we can be is not self–centered. Failure in self–leadership causes us to flirt with anxiety, frustration, stress, confusion, and burnout. Marriages and families are neglected. Physical bodies are ignored. We begin to major on minors. We lose any sense of joy and meaning. Unable to lead ourselves, we're ineffective in leading others. At best, we're running on fumes. When that happens we're reminded that Scripture calls us to be living sacrifices, not dead ones (Romans 12:1)!

Personally, I fear I've missed a lot of joy along the way because of misunderstandings and confusion about who God created me to be. Knowing my time on this earth is growing shorter by the minute, I find myself regretting time I may have spent on "good" things at the expense of the "better" things God may have intended for me all along. Truth is, I suspect that's true of many of us. After all, it's not hard to spot the glazed looks and just going through the motions of life that characterize too many of us. Then, factor in our hardheaded resistance to submission to God's plan for our life. Is it any wonder that so many of us flounder through life trying to convince ourselves that life holds more meaning than what we're experiencing now?

The NICHE model in the pages that follow represents my attempt to find answers for myself for two of the really weighty questions of life all of us struggle with: Who am I and why am I here? In the midst of my journey, I discovered one overarching life principle: *There's no need for us to be like anyone or better than anyone as long as we're the best "us" we can be.*

From reading Scripture, I'm convinced even Jesus spent a great deal of time exploring these two greater questions of life. Similarly, discovering our NICHE is a proactive, intentional walk that only we can take for ourselves. As one who continues that trek daily, I can assure you it's worth the trip!

THE BACK STORY

> "… being confident of this, that he who began a good work in you will carry it on to completion until the day of Christ Jesus."
>
> (Philippians 1:6)

I'll always recall it as "the day the lights went out". That's really the only way I know to describe what was happening to me that morning. It was as if someone had thrown a switch that totally extinguished any semblance of joy and contentment I had known not so long ago. One more request by a totally innocent church member was all it took to send me reeling over the edge.

There I was, a Christian man in my mid–forties, happily–married to a lady I absolutely adored and considered my best friend. Janie and I had all the basic creature comforts we needed. I was comfortable in my career. Many of my minister friends would have given their right arm to serve in the church and with the staff I saw every day. Life couldn't have been any better, could it? So, what was going on?

If I was honest with myself, I would have admitted I could see this "power failure" coming for some time. Maybe I had been guilty of attempting to do too many things — and doing none of them

particularly well. Oh, I was busy, but it was always with a vague sense that I was working harder and longer with little to show for my efforts. I kept asking myself, "Is this all there is?" It became harder to drag myself out of bed each morning to face another day just like the day before and the day before that. My enthusiasm and passion had been misplaced somewhere along the way. Now, I had been knocked to my knees with the realization that the charade was over. I could no longer fool myself or others. I had hit rock bottom!

Over time, I had begun taking my spiritual connection with God for granted. Yes, that happens to ministers, too! Rather foolishly, I was attempting to do too much in my own strength and wisdom. I found myself becoming a person I was never created to be and trying to do things I was never called or gifted to do. Too many others — and certainly not God — were pulling the strings in my life. More than not being on the same page with God, we weren't even reading from the same book!

As is true with many others in our 24/7/365 world, I was feeling the strain in every facet of my life. But, that I found myself in this situation was totally my fault. By allowing myself to be consumed by the busyness of life and ministry, I had lost touch with God in some fundamental ways. I needed to slow down, take a step back, and spend some time reflecting.

Now, for the first time in a long time, I found myself seeking God and his vision for the next steps of my life and ministry. I longed for that contentment with myself and the fulfillment I had known once before. Looking back, my one regret is that I was over forty years into life and almost twenty years into my ministry career before I embarked on my journey.

The Journey Begins

To guide my journey, I began praying, reading, and writing to find a way out of this dark hole I found myself in. Many recall

Rick Warren, pastor of Saddleback Church in Orange County, California, writing a book in 1995 entitled *The Purpose Driven Church*. In that book, Warren introduced the SHAPE acrostic (Spiritual gifts, Heart/passion, Abilities, Personality, Experiences) to guide persons in determining what their ministry in and through their church should be.

Being aware of the SHAPE acrostic and using that as my starting point, I crafted my own acrostic using the word NICHE.

N – atural bent
I – ndividual personality
C – harismata, or spiritual gifts
H – eart, or passion
E – xperiences/accomplishment

But, as I began my search, I had a deeper purpose in mind. I was attempting to figure out, not just what I was to DO with the remainder of my life, but who God had created me to BE in the first place. My quest was about reconnecting with and getting to know better the One who created me. Then, based on that knowledge, I could better determine where I fit in. Where was my NICHE?

And, I began teaching and sharing what I was discovering. Surprisingly (or perhaps not!), I found my journey resonated with that of others. The questions I found myself asking seemed to be the same questions those in all stages of their spiritual pilgrimage, believers and unbelievers alike, were posing.

One of my great passions is for Christians and unbelievers to discover the life God intended for them, to live it with passion and few regrets. I can assure you many of our family, friends, business colleagues, students, and church members are looking for just that. They're seeking answers to the same questions I found myself asking. So, what I propose is not just a compass for our own contentment and fulfillment. It's meant to offer guidance for those in our circle of acquaintances who have the same longing.

Now, I don't claim to be all-knowing or all-seeing, able to delve in to the recesses of a person's life and tell you just what they're experiencing. But, I have learned there are clues we can look for. Maybe we see it in their eyes or the way they carry themselves. Where is the enthusiasm and passion we once heard in their voice? They still attempt to put on a strong face for others. But, the unmistakable, unspoken message is that this isn't the life they imagined or signed on for. We know they're losing their way.

I will not promise you that time spent on this journey will wrap up God's path for our life in a neat little package with a ribbon on top of it. In fact, I'm not sure we can ever say with certainty and finality, "This is my NICHE. This is God's specific plan and direction for the rest of my life." Too many things change along the way – our health, interests, relationships, opportunities. We'll pass through new seasons of life.

Though I have more answers than when I began, I'm still on the journey. But, the real fun is in the discoveries along the way, not in the destination. At this point, we can't know all God is doing and wants to do in and through our life. We may have to revisit and adjust our NICHE. But one certainty you and I can hold on to as we make the journey — God didn't create us simply to exist on earth before entering real life in heaven. We are placed here in this specific period of human history for a purpose. We're part of the story God is writing.

I don't know how ordinary or extraordinary your life is, but you have a part to play. You may insist, "I'm just a mom/dad/student/ grandparent/employee, a minister in a small church, a Sunday school teacher, etc." The list goes on and on to describe how ordinary our existence sometimes seems to be. Yet, we don't know and can't know this side of heaven how significant our part of the story can be.

Guideposts for the Journey

As I began to delve in to my NICHE and putting the pieces together, I discovered some truths to keep in mind. Finding our NICHE is not:

- **Self–serving.** Some would have us believe discovering God's will is to determine what *we* most want to do— and then do just the opposite. But, God isn't that consummate killjoy some imagine him to be. Where in Scripture does God ever say we're not to wholeheartedly enjoy life, left to simply trudge through our allotted time on earth, just going through the motions? God created us for that kind of meaning and fulfillment that will draw others to him. You and I were made to know abundant life (more about that in a moment). Of course, whether or not we access that offer is, ultimately, up to us.
- **Not about *us* conceiving a plan for our life.** Many people do choose a path for life based on their own life's agenda, only to pay the price in boredom, frustration, discouragement, fatigue, and mediocrity. God never intended that for us. In Jeremiah 29:11, we read, "For I know the plans I have for you," declares the Lord, "plans to prosper you and not to harm you, plans to give you hope and a future?" God is the author of a plan for our life that results in contentment and meaning.
- **Only about finding the right career path.** Discovering our NICHE, will impact not only our career, but our family and personal life. In reality, it's a spiritual trek more than anything else. Living out of our NICHE is about making the *whole* of life worth living.
- **Only about us.** We can be certain of one fact — God's best plan for us will involve others. That's why Jesus emphasized,

"whoever wants to be great among you must be your servant." (Matthew 20:26)

In a chapter she wrote for *Christian Reflections on the Leadership Challenge* by James M. Kouzes and Barry Z. Posner, Nancy Ortberg clarifies the essence of servant leadership:

> Jesus did not talk about leadership very often, and every time he did, he talked about serving. When Jesus served people, he called for them to turn their lives upside down. He was constantly going for the deeper motivations and the part in them that was created in the image of God – the part that says, "I can be more than this." He didn't just walk around getting coffee for people and patting them on the back. That's not what it means to serve. Serving means that when this person leaves my leadership sphere of influence, he or she will be a better person and leader because of the time spent with me.

And, again, quoting Reggie McNeal, "True greatness is realized through servanthood that helps people become more than what they have been, maybe even more than they thought they could be." Speaking for myself, there is no greater joy than seeing the light go on in someone's eyes, perhaps for the first time, as they realize, "This is what I was made for!"

Conversely, finding our NICHE is.

- **Determining how God made us** — and finding, perhaps for the first time, we enjoy being the real us! The need for play acting or trying to be someone we were never meant to be simply goes away.

- **Realizing we no longer need to compare ourselves with others**. When you arrive in heaven, what question do you think God will ask? "How many did you bring with you? Why couldn't you be more like Billy Graham or Mother Teresa?" I really don't think we'll be asked any of those. More likely, I expect this question from God: "What did you do with the relationships and opportunities I gave you?"

    Our NICHE is about realizing that God's purpose for us is a unique, one-of-a-kind design. No one else has our interests, roles, abilities, opportunities, and relationships. Each of us is created to live at this specific time in history and in our own "little corner of the world". If we don't invest ourselves there, who will be the influence God intended if not us?

    No longer do you and I feel the need to measure our lives by what we see happening in the lives of others. The challenge is to be the person we were meant to be and find contentment in that. Gratitude for who God created us to be is a sure antidote to the constant temptation to compare ourselves and our life with others. We become less concerned about the expectations of others. Rather than being consumed with that which we "ought to do" or "have to do", we will discover we can make a difference by doing what we "want to do" for God.

- **About moving beyond a life of drudgery and mediocrity**. Bill Bright, founder of Campus Crusade for Christ, used to tell a story of a traveler who realized a lifelong dream and bought a ticket on a cruise ship. He, then, endured three weeks of eating cheese crackers while watching fellow passengers make their way to the dining room to enjoy prime rib and lobster. Somehow he had missed that meals were included with the price of the cruise.

    Sadly, he's not at all unlike too many who have purchased their ticket for heaven and don't realize all that's included.

Don't be misled. Life lived in a broken world isn't always prime rib and lobster. Christians experience the hard times in life, too. But, Jesus' offer of abundant life helps us to see them as mere speed bumps along the way to something beyond the endless drudgery of life.

God didn't create us only for eternity and heaven. He designed us for a life of meaning and fulfillment here and now. When he suggests we can know life "to the full" or "abundant", he doesn't mean just a little joy, or slightly blessed, or partially fulfilled. He means to give us the whole boatload, even though that's just a taste of what heaven has in store.

- **Is about finding a way to make a difference in OUR world.** Determining who God created us to be and what he made us to do is about more than simply knowing a comfortable existence. There's nothing necessarily wrong with that. But, our gut feeling is that the promises and even the luxuries of this world won't be enough to really satisfy us. The genuine purpose, meaning, and contentment *all of us* seek are realized when we get beyond concern only for ourselves and invest ourselves in others.

Author and motivational speaker Zig Ziglar makes an audacious, but so very true claim. "You can get everything in life you want if you help enough people get what they want." Why else are so many today opting for a second career or choosing early retirement just to get out of this rat race we call "success"? It's not that success is bad; it just isn't enough. A life lived totally for self and accumulation of "stuff" fails to survive much longer than our lifespan. The real joy is in a life's investment in others that outlives us. Consciously or not, we long to live a life that counts, to make a difference in our world.

What began as a mini—crisis for me became a watershed experience in my life. At the time, I recalled some advice I'd received years earlier from a counselor friend. "Gary, under God, take control of your life — or someone else will." With that counsel ringing in my ears, I began my journey toward a new lease on life and ministry, one that would affect me personally, professionally, emotionally, and, most of all, spiritually. So, with these guidelines in mind, let's get started on this journey! Strangely enough, mine began with an insight from my experiences on the golf course.

CHAPTER 1

SEEKING OUR "SWEET SPOT"

If you've played very much golf at all, you've heard about the "sweet spot". It's that moment to be savored when golfer, swing, golf ball, and club all come together. The result is a picture–perfect swing, the kind you only read about in *Golf Digest*. The swing is perfect; the hands feel no vibration as club crushes ball. The ball travels where it was meant to go — and goes a long way. You've hit the sweet spot!

Let me assure you there is a "sweet spot" in your life and in mine. It's that point when who we are — our abilities, personality, and passion — intersects with God's purpose and plan for us. The end result is a sense of meaningful life, contentment, and significance. We're living the life for which we are created. In short, it's that quality of life all of us long for.

But, let's be honest. Just as finding the sweet spot on a golf club requires tremendous eye–hand coordination, realizing our personal sweet spot doesn't happen by accident. How many of us, at some point in life, find ourselves asking questions like these?

- Is the life I live now all there is?
- What's the point?
- What do I do with myself for the rest of my life?

We desperately long for something more than trite answers for those questions. Because, as Christian researcher George Barna reminds us, "Sadly, there is one fact we all will deal with eventually — there are no "do–overs" in life!"

So This Is "Meaning"?

From all outward appearances, there are some among us who seemingly enjoy a life of great meaning, even success. But when questioned, even some of those confess their own sense of emptiness and frustration. Science fiction novelist Isaac Asimov once stated, "As far as I can see there is no purpose to life."

Surely author Mark Twain could find some measure of meaning in life. But the sentiment expressed shortly before his death reveals the task was beyond even this gifted wordsmith.

> A myriad of men are born; they labor and sweat and struggle; ... they squabble and scold and fight; they scramble for little mean advantages over each other; age creeps upon them; infirmities follow; ... those they love are taken from them, and the joy of life is turned to aching grief. It (the release) comes at last —the only unpoisoned gift earth ever had for them — and they vanish from a world where they were of no consequence, a world which will lament them a day and forget them forever.

Now, there's a reason to get out of bed in the morning!

Or consider the globe–trotting style of Ernest Hemingway. Big–game hunter, war correspondent, lover of good times, Hemingway was married four times and lived with reckless abandon. About his life, he said, "I live in a vacuum that is as lonely as a radio tube when the batteries are dead, and there is no current to plug into."

One Sunday morning in Idaho, he ended it all with a shotgun blast to the head.

Tennis star Boris Becker was at the very top of the tennis world, yet he was on the brink of suicide. He confessed, "I had won Wimbledon twice before, once as the youngest player. I was rich. I had all the material possessions I needed ... It's the old song of movie stars and pop stars who commit suicide. They have everything, and yet they are so unhappy. I had no inner peace. I was a puppet on a string." Finally, actor James Dean's favorite saying reflected his understanding of life's purpose: "Live fast, die young, and leave a good–looking corpse."

Still, one of the saddest summations of our human existence was penned by noted author and Christian apologist, C.S. Lewis. "We are half–hearted creatures, fooling around with drink, sex and ambition when infinite joy is offered us, like an ignorant child who wants to go on making mud pies in a slum because he can't imagine what is meant by the offer of a holiday at the sea."

The tragic truth is that we can live for the sole purpose of indulging ourselves and survive quite nicely. No question, we can accomplish much apart from God and maybe even benefit others. But will it be enough? Is that the "purposeful" living to which we aspire? Can we really label our life a "success" when built on a foundation of one or more of the following?

Affluence

Fans of the American Wild West will find in a Deadwood, South Dakota museum this inscription left by a beleaguered prospector: "I lost my gun. I lost my horse. I am out of food. The Indians are after me. But I've got all the gold I can carry."

Our culture, like those through the ages, is in the midst of a love affair with money and the things it can buy. Call it, if you will, an "affliction with affluence". But, let's be honest about one thing. Though we may not be able to buy the meaning and joy in life we long for so much, money can buy a whole lot of fleeting happiness.

For too many of us, the size of a bank account, house, or car are the defining measure of who we are in the eyes of others and ourselves. Our "wants" escalate to become "needs" easily satisfied just by plunking down a credit card. If we can only get enough! But how much is enough?

Wealth tends to blind us to our need for God and creates the fantasy of self–sufficiency, that we somehow control our very existence and future. Hear the conclusion of King Solomon, one who had all the money he wanted or needed. "Whoever loves money never has money enough; whoever loves wealth is never satisfied with his income. This too is meaningless." (Ecclesiastes 5:10) Solomon took a peek down the road of life to see how this desperate pursuit of money played out. "Naked a man comes from his mother's womb, and as he comes, so he departs. He takes nothing from his labor that he can carry in his hand." (Ecclesiastes 5:15) Plenty of money and things, but Solomon's life remained empty.

Money, itself, isn't the problem. There's no real virtue in being poor. To have money and lots of it isn't a sin as long as it doesn't become the all–or–nothing god of our life. But, it's as if we assess personal value by economic worth. Meanwhile, the rat race continues and we're no nearer the finish line than the poorest among us.

Interestingly, American psychologist and highly–regarded business management thinker Frederick Herzberg compiled results of studies of individuals in a variety of work situations in the mid–twentieth century. He concluded that salary, alone, isn't enough to provide satisfaction for workers. All the salary does is decrease the likelihood of dissatisfaction in the workplace. To foster real satisfaction and optimism, another set of "motivator factors" must be considered. These factors acknowledge an individual's need for

personal growth and include status and recognition, opportunity for advancement, being viewed as a responsible individual, challenging and stimulating work, and a sense of personal achievement and growth.

For example, appreciation for a job well done may well trump salary as a motivator, causing some to insist, "Without appreciation for who I am and what I do, you couldn't pay me enough to be work here!" In fact, in his book, *The Top Ten Mistakes Leaders Make*, leadership author Hans Finzel notes, "Organizational researchers have been telling us for years that affirmation motivates people much more than financial incentives, but we still don't get it."

Amusement

Pure pleasure is one chosen path to joy in life for many. It's not really the worst path we could take. No question there's fun and pleasure to be had in life. But like much this world offers, pure pleasure is no cure–all. The greater problem with pleasure is that, once we've had a taste, we want more!

A few years ago, Janie and I took our first cruise in the Bahamas. The weather was perfect and the water as clear and blue–green as any picture postcard. A full moon was ours as we walked the deck after dinner. We enjoyed first–class accommodations and food that seemed to appear twenty four hours a day. A highlight of the week was snorkeling at a private desert island. We lay in a hammock under the palms. In short, for pure pleasure, we had it all for a few short days. Gilligan should have it so good! I highly recommend a cruise!

But, just three years later, we took the same cruise with an added stop in Key West. Before we left, anticipation was high. But, you guessed it. Nice as that second cruise was (and it was nice!), the thrill, the pure pleasure simply couldn't be duplicated.

Our experience illustrates the deceit of pleasure. That which satisfied before will, in time, become almost boring and tiresome,

too. More exotic locations and more exhilarating diversions are required to get the same thrill. Meanwhile, the quest for the ultimate kick leaves in its wake wasted time, talents, and opportunities.

Again, the delusion is as old as King Solomon. This lavishly wealthy man, with the whole world at his beck and call, denied himself no pleasure and spared no expense. Having it all, what was his conclusion? "Come now, I will test you with pleasure to find out what is good. But that also proved to be meaningless." (Ecclesiastes 2:1)

Accomplishment

There's every reason to celebrate when we move up the career ladder, complete our education, have something we wrote published, or realize some other personal goal. But, in time, regardless of the accomplishment, we're likely to be brought back to earth. We haven't yet arrived. There's always room for growth; further goals await.

I recall completion of my doctoral studies. After four and one half long years of seminars, research, papers, examinations, a written dissertation, and unrelenting deadlines, there came that sweet day in July 1986. Just as I dreamed it would someday happen, I heard for the first time those words from my program supervisor, "Congratulations, Dr. Chapman".

But weeks later, I became despondent, wondering why I had pursued the degree at all. Later, I learned my response wasn't that unusual for post–doctoral students. What made the difference for me was to "get back in the game". It was time to move on to other dreams and goals.

The absence of goals in life can lead to burnout and/or depression. We need those goals to keep us going. Jim Collins, business consultant and author of *Good to Great*, reminds us, "The moment you think of yourself as great, your slide toward mediocrity will have already begun." We can never afford to recline on past

accomplishment. There's always some other goal of value and influence we can pursue. No single accomplishment is the final benchmark of godly success. It's only one measure at best.

Authority

"If I could just be in charge!" We envy those who have authority and imagine what it would be like to occupy the corner office or have our name listed on the top rung of the organizational hierarchy. To have people jump at our command, be accountable to no one for our decisions, and shape the future as we see fit, is the ultimate power trip. In our mind, we judge success by how many people respond to our bidding.

Most of us imagine that, given the opportunity, we could wield authority well. But all too often power has an almost intoxicating effect, degenerating into bullying and manipulation. There is a great difference between being "the boss" and being a leader of genuine influence. Real leadership is influence earned by serving others, being sensitive to their needs, and guiding them to achieve their God–given potential. To view persons as little more than a means for accomplishing our own goals is a faulty view of leadership fostered by a self–centered world.

Authority is a wonderful tool in the hands of one who understands Jesus' words. "Instead, whoever wants to become great among you must be your servant, and whoever wants to be first must be slave of all." (Mark 10:43–44) He also modeled what he preached. This same man who asserted, "All authority in heaven and on earth has been given to me." (Matthew 28:18) is the same man who earlier washed the feet of his own disciples.

The influence we long for with others is not produced by feeling superior or insisting on personal privilege. Those we gladly follow are real leaders who exercise authority even as they show concern for our well–being and attempt to bring out the best in us. Again, Jesus

is our model. He didn't just point the way to a life of significance. He offered to take us with him! That's servant leadership at its best.

Acclaim

Let me invite you to spend a moment in an especially revealing little memory exercise. Think back now. Remember who the popular kids were in your high school class? If you're like me, you might be able to picture some of their faces. Depending on how long ago you graduated, you may have to go back to the yearbook, though, to even recall their names.

That little trek down memory lane illustrates the fleeting nature of popularity and the acclaim that goes with it. So often, what little adulation we or others enjoyed in high school was based on "what have you done for me lately?" That really doesn't change all that much, even as adults. There were some pretty popular athletes, music groups, and movie stars just a few years ago. But mention those names to today's adolescents, and likely they'll respond, "Who's that?"

We all desire acceptance and the esteem of peers. It's natural to do so and, as long as we don't dishonor God or us, there's nothing wrong with that. Still, popularity and the acclaim of others are fleeting at best unless there's some more significant influence. As a lasting yardstick of the real fulfillment we desire, it's never quite enough.

* * *

There's nothing wrong with any of these pursuits. But, alone or together, none are the key that opens the door to the meaningful life we seek. Any satisfaction we derive will be short-lived. Before long, we'll be trolling the same waters looking for the same kind of fulfillment. So, is there another path to the life we really desire? I'm glad you asked!

LIFE COACHING QUESTIONS

- *Who are the "thieves" in YOUR midst that promise so much in life, but are guilty of not delivering?*

Now That's What I'm Talking About!

Upfront, let me share a couple of disclaimers. First of all, what I'm about to share is based on my personal faith journey with God. That same journey may or may not be yours. Just be assured I'm not attempting, in any way, to impose my faith. That's simply the perspective from which I write and it's impossible for me to share my journey apart from my trust in God. Life just makes more sense for me when God is at the core. That may not be the case for you. And yet, whether God is significant for your life or not, I do believe any of us will readily see the application of the lessons I'll share.

Secondly, in what follows, there is probably little that qualifies as ground–breaking. Instead, I'm simply trying to develop a step–by–step approach for better understanding the person God created us to be and what he called us to do. In doing so, I offer little in the way of scientific assessments. I'll leave that for the psychologists and trained counselors. Instead, I simply share the account of a fellow pilgrim seeking some degree of lasting joy and contentment in my life.

I suppose some of where I found myself that day years ago may have been related to what is typically referred to as midlife crisis. But, I had a sense there was more to it than that. Soon, my journey became a spiritual quest to become more the man God created me to be and to determine how God would have me spend the remainder of my life. And, I wanted to live with passion and enthusiasm. I wanted to look forward to every new day. Simply playing out the string was not an option for me.

Over time, a new bud of life began to peek through the frozen ground for me. Being based on Scripture, I know some may resist

this notion as being too "religious". But, I'm convinced Jesus looked down through the centuries to anticipate some of the very questions I and others are asking about meaning and contentment in life. In response, he offered what he called "abundant life". That became the focal point for my search.

> Therefore Jesus said again, "Very truly I tell you, I am the gate for the sheep. All who have come before me are thieves and robbers, but the sheep have not listened to them. I am the gate; whoever enters through me will be saved. They will come in and go out, and find pasture. The thief comes only to steal and kill and destroy; I have come that they may have life, and have it to the full. (John 10:7–10)

Understand the background of what Jesus is saying. Each time he traveled to Jerusalem, Jesus encountered more and more hostility from religious leaders. Much of the opposition stemmed from the fact that the religious leaders refused to be the spiritual shepherds the people needed —and Jesus was not at all reluctant to call them on it. In a society where sheep were such a vital part of lifestyle and economy, he used an easily understood analogy to describe his mission and the shortcomings of the religious leaders.

The sheepfold would have only one gate. A conscientious shepherd would sleep in front of it at night to protect his sheep. In describing himself as "the gate for the sheep", Jesus is saying, "I am the one 'door' to the sheepfold that will provide true security and contentment for the sheep." By contrast, Jesus pointed to the religious leaders who pursue their own agenda and reveal no real concern for others. They exploit their "sheep" and don't think twice about destroying them to further their own cause.

On this particular occasion, Jesus makes an emphatic distinction between the life he offers and the promises of life this world offers. The word Jesus used for "life" is *zoen*, a depth and quality of life meaning more than ordinary physical existence *(bios)*. To be honest

I don't know that Jesus is suggesting we must forfeit *bios* in order to have *zoen*. But, a fabulous career, a new home in the right part of town, designer clothes, a company car, vacations, and physical attractiveness won't be enough. Real life, *zoen*, the life we're really seeking, is spiritual more than physical. Hard as we try to convince ourselves otherwise, the life we most long for is all about God.

Digging a little deeper, we discover the Greek word for "abundantly" (*perisson*) pictures an endless, overflowing container or spring of water. It's true, most of us tend to expect too much of life this side of heaven. Still, Jesus is offering us, here and now, at least a foretaste of the life that will be ours in eternity.

Question is, how do I experience this abundant life for myself? Why do we have such a difficult time taking God up on his offer of abundant life? It certainly doesn't happen by accident. To actually experience for ourselves the life Christ offers requires a proactive choice on our part to receive this truly once–in–a–lifetime offer. And, there's the rub. *Zoen* begins with trusting our Creator to provide us with a life far richer than we could imagine or achieve on our own. Now, we're talking submission.

CHAPTER 2

WHO'S IN YOUR COCKPIT?

Picture your life as the cockpit of a 787 airliner. When we allow our life to be open to God's leading, his Holy Spirit comes on board with us. He's in the cockpit with us. But the central feature of this cockpit is the pilot's seat. From that chair, all the decisions are made about the path of our life. Those decisions will shape the person we will become, how we live, and yes, whether we will know abundant life or not.

Whoever is in the chair makes the decisions. Now, I can't speak for you. But, my natural inclination and arrogant human nature lead me, on many occasions, to trust myself, more than God, to chart the path of my life. That attitude, alone, is the epitome of our sinful nature. Too often, we relegate Christ to a corner of the cockpit. "Spirit of God, I'm glad to have you on board with me. But right now I'm doing okay. You just stand over there in the corner and if I need you, I'll call." Having him in our life provides some peace. But to yield total control to him is another matter. Then we marvel at how often we "crash and burn" when left to make our own decisions.

When we trust our future to Jesus, our eternal destiny is sealed; we are, now and forevermore, part of God's family. Yet, critical as that decision may be, our salvation has a present dimension, too. Some believers are so preoccupied with life after death that we

neglect God's intent for life here and now, one as full as we can know short of eternity with God in heaven.

But let me be very upfront here. Accessing abundant life is difficult for us for one simple reason and one only. *How we struggle with submission to anyone or anything, including God.* It's a seemingly bizarre notion that runs counter to the self-reliant mindset of our culture. We may be willing to acknowledge God as our Creator and Savior. Maybe. The harder choice for us is allowing him control of our day to day existence.

Biblical submission often gets an unfairly bad rap. Keep in mind, though, we're not talking about submission to a religion, church, or body of doctrine. And it's not as if we have no choice but blind surrender. Rather, it's a reasoned choice to trust our daily existence to God, based on a history of him coming through for us in the past. More specifically, this submission is not a one-time decision to trust God. Each and every situation we encounter creates another choice for us — will I submit this time, too? Biblical submission is day by day, moment by moment obedience to a God who loves us more than we can imagine and wants only the best for us.

True confession: Now in the latter stages of life, I fear I've missed much abundant life simply because of my desire to be in control. But, ironic as it may seem, I'm beginning to understand that I am most free to be all I can be when I finally do submit to God's direction. I can do it my way and know, perhaps, some of the comfort and pleasure of this life. But, more often than not, I end up feeling more frustrated, stressed, anxious, and overwhelmed than joyous. The wiser move is for me to step back in to that submissive relationship with God.

Abundant living happens as a byproduct of life in the Spirit. We access this longed-for joy only by submitting to the control of God's Spirit in our life. "I give up, Lord. I've tried it my way. Please take your rightful place in the pilot's seat."

Whose Dream Are We Chasing?

The whole issue of realizing the abundant life Jesus offers leads to still another question I've had to struggle with from time to time. That is, whose dream am I pursuing, God's vision for me or my own misguided "daydreams"? Am I open to the very best possible life path God has in mind for me? Or, will I insist on doing it my way, perhaps bringing God along for the ride to, hopefully, bless the path I choose?

In order to pursue all God has in mind for us, I've learned that it's likely we have to give up some or all of our own dreams of what our life's path might, could, or should look like. Not always, but more often than not, that is the reality we struggle with. And doing so may not be an altogether bad thing.

For example, I recall a time in my late teens and early twenties when I toyed with the idea of a career as a professional golfer. Assuming I had the ability to play professional golf and make a living (a big assumption to be sure), I envisioned a career path that could have worked out well for me. And I have no doubt God could have used golf as a platform for serving him and others.

But, reflecting now, I suspect there would have been an ongoing pesky suspicion that I had missed God's best for me. I may have been reasonably satisfied, enjoying a comfortable life, experiencing moments of enjoyment and accomplishment. But, somewhere along the way would I have sensed missing something I couldn't quite put my finger on?

Even now, I look back at almost forty years of ministry, a tenure with a lot of peaks and valleys. In spite of its ups and downs, its good side and not so good side, I wouldn't choose any other life's path. That doesn't mean I don't have regrets or wouldn't do some things differently. But, looking back, I'm convinced this is the best God had in mind for me. God has called me to and allowed me to experience more than I could have imagined. He's taken me on a path I never imagined possible. While a career as a professional golfer may have

seemed appealing at the time, in hindsight it seems almost laughable and so very inadequate. I'm glad I didn't miss all God had in store.

Consider the apostle Peter. Early on, Peter may have imagined he would always be a fisherman. He was good at it, too. I don't know how passionate he was about fishing or if it was just a way to make a living. In any case, God had something else — something more meaningful — in mind. As Peter neared the end of his life, can we really picture him looking back with regret that he hadn't remained a fisherman? Granted, tradition says Peter was martyred because of his willingness to follow Jesus. But, my suspicion is that he would make the same decision to follow Jesus every time! For some, fishing may have been enough. But not for Peter!

I'm not suggesting the best and only path God has in mind for any of us is a life of full–time professional ministry. Far from it! God may very well be charting a life's path for you that includes professional golf, fishing, or some other pursuit. That may be the "best" he has in mind for you. All I'm suggesting is that we be willing to sacrifice our dreams for his better dream.

Keep in mind, too, that discovering our NICHE is not only about us. We are fashioned by a Creator who has every right to determine how we can best be used for a Kingdom purpose. Thankfully, our Creator has more than our simply existing for a too brief time on earth. Instead, he designs us with a purpose that, not only impacts others, but brings us meaning and satisfaction. Problem is, we can hold on so long to an unrealistic dream that we miss the open door right before us.

So, there may come a time when we have to give up on an improbable goal. All of us know how difficult it is to give up an ambition that's been a part of us for so long. In my case, it was fairly easy to go in another direction. After all, I soon realized I simply didn't have the talent for professional golf. The alternative would have been a life spent in denial and frustration pursuing a pipedream I'd never realize.

Worthy as our dream may be, wouldn't it be more reasonable to align our own will with God's purpose for creating us (his call on our life) and move on to a more realistic and meaningful aspiration? Assuming we have a desire to seek God's will rather than our own, we covenant to live life God's way. We do so confident in God's promise of abundant life and with assurance that he has something even better in mind for us. We come to the end of life with more satisfaction and fewer regrets.

What's In It for Me?

So, assuming God could really provide you and me with that taste of eternity here and now, what would that mean for us? What does Jesus' offer of abundant life have to do with our quest for the sweet spot in life? How would we be closer to discovering our NICHE if Jesus' abundant life became reality for us?

Again, I can't speak for others. But, in the context of my own search, I knew that abundant living would encompass, at the very least, the following four qualities, all of which represent the essence of a life lived in the "sweet spot"

> *Day–to–Day Contentment* In contrast to those who dread each new day and can't seem to find their way out of bed, God and his purpose in life instills a passion, a reason for living. We can't help looking forward to each new day, no matter how routine and repetitive the events on our to–do list appear to be. Contentment means I'm free to be me and glad to be me. When I lay my head on the pillow tonight, I will do so knowing I did the best I could with this day. There's no fretting about what might have been. In the words of the apostle Paul, "I am not saying this because I am in need, for I have learned to be content whatever the circumstances." (Philippians 4:11).

Enduring Fulfillment

> After spending millions of dollars and experiencing loss of life among their fellow climbers, two men finally reached the peak of Mount Everest. There, at the top, they viewed the world from its highest point. They had overcome enormous obstacles to reach their destination, their ultimate goal, yet the emotion they experienced was not one of unadulterated elation and joyfulness. After just a few minutes, one of them began worrying about how to get down the other side before the wind blew them off the top of the mountain. – Bob Buford in *Halftime*

Ever wonder if, as we near the end of life, that we'll feel our life's accomplishments weren't enough? That there's something else out there — we just don't know what — and now it's too late?

On the other hand, wouldn't it be great to be able to have placed on our tombstone the words, "No Regrets"? Though all of us will, likely, look back with a few "what if's", enduring fulfillment means my life was spent just about as well as it could be.

Hope In The Midst of Difficult Circumstances But, content and fulfilled as we may be, life often throws us a curveball. In 2008, my dad died after a prolonged battle with cancer. There is no one in this world who has ever been a greater model for me. I lost one of my best friends that day. My heart was crushed. Still, on the day of his funeral, I was able to stand and voice words of praise for God and joy for my dad. No longer would he be in pain; I knew exactly where he was and that I would see him again. God had taken him home! That's joy!

You and I can't create or manufacture lasting joy on our own. At the time of my dad's death, all I had to fall back on was God and his grace. But, at the time, it was enough. Joy is realized when God shows up. And, when he does arrive, you know it! God's joy overcomes even the worst circumstances of life.

God doesn't promise unlimited joy and unceasing blessing simply because we consider ourselves to be a Christian. Sometimes, we must endure circumstances that represent anything but joy. Still, I've experienced on many occasions that my love relationship with God puts me in position to know his joy – in spite of circumstances. As we grow in our relationship with God, we find ourselves experiencing joy in the most difficult of circumstances.

Lasting Legacy How we desire to be remembered by those who follow us is the truest yardstick of how we define what it is to live with satisfaction and significance. It is the path our life will take if we have the impact we'd most like to have in those persons nearest and dearest to us.

We all dream how our world, our community, our churches, our families, and our friends might be different because of our life's contribution. That's why American philosopher William James stated, "The great use of life is to spend it for something that will outlast it." As Christians, we may not dread or fear death. Our bigger fear is to come to the end of life having never really lived at all!

With those objectives in mind, I found myself seeking my place, my NICHE, in this divine drama that was unfolding around me. The word, "niche", seemed appropriate to describe my quest. Merriam–Webster defines "niche" as "a place, employment, status, or activity for which a person or thing is best fitted". Implied is a recognition that each of us have a unique niche based on who we

are, our created qualities, our interests, and so on. To be honest, though, to this point I was feeling like that proverbial square peg being crammed in to a round hole. My search was for that niche that fit me more naturally. I was hoping to discover answers for God's will for the remainder of my life, to better understand why he created me at all, and to know more than mediocre existence.

All things considered, with Jesus' offer of abundant life on the table for any and all of us, it is my conviction that it would be sin for me to know anything less. I would be failing God and myself to be merely average, to be satisfied to simply get by when God has called me to something greater. In fact, I have long insisted the worst thing you can say about me as a Christ–follower is that I'm just like everyone else!

LIFE COACHING QUESTIONS

- *How would you explain to a friend that abundant life in Christ is the life they've been seeking all along? How would you explain that this life is worth the cost?*
- *When you hear that Jesus offers abundant life, what does that suggest for you?*

You Surely Don't Mean Me!

> "I praise you because I am fearfully and wonderfully made; your works are wonderful, I know that full well."
>
> (Psalm 139:14)

I can just hear some arguing, though:

- "Surely you're talking about somebody else!"

- "God couldn't have had me in mind when he talked about abundant life."
- "I'm so ordinary. I've always been told I would never amount to much or make anything of myself."

Those are some of the negative messages we receive from teachers, coaches, parents, friends, ministers, maybe even ourselves. Hear that often enough and we actually begin to believe the self–fulfilling prophecy.

But how would God respond to those comments about us? What does God see when he looks at each and every one of us? Does he not see a unique creation, a person created in his own image? Would he not point to any of us and proclaim us "top–of–the–line, first class"?

It's true, each of us are different. But variety is just God's way of reminding us, "You're one of a kind — just as I intended when I created you." God is not limited by family tree, background, social standing, economic condition, education or lack of it, race, gender, etc.

Imagine, for example, someone offered you a dirty, crumpled one hundred dollar bill. Would you throw it away because of where it's been and what it looks like now? Of course not! It's still worth one hundred dollars, even if it's held together with scotch tape. That's how God sees us! In spite of my efforts to prove my love for God and earn his love for me, he already loves me more than I could ever imagine. He's not nearly so concerned about where we've been as where we're going. He is the God of clean slates and second chances. Nothing we have ever done or ever will do can change God's love for us, his appraisal of our value, or the possibilities he had in mind when he created us. That's grace! Created in the image of God, why should we allow another person to determine how valuable we are? Instead, allow God to determine our value.

For example, let me tell you about Aunt Mae. As a four or five year old boy in a church in the mountains of North Carolina, Aunt

Mae was my Sunday school teacher. She really wasn't my aunt and I don't know why everybody called her that; she was just Aunt Mae.

Aunt Mae loved us children. Her arms made for some great hugs and, when we needed comforting, there was no better place to be than in her lap. She dearly loved us and made us feel loved. And we loved her.

I remember when I heard the news years later that Aunt Mae had died. It was like a part of me had died, too. Because, more than half a century later, I remember Aunt Mae. As unknown and unremarkable as she may have been, she was a difference maker for at least one little boy.

Each and every one of us was created for that kind of life's meaning. Regardless of the part I have in the story, I just want to come to the end of life and hear Jesus say, "Well done, faithful servant. You took the stage and played your part well."

CHAPTER 3

N-ATURAL BENT

Ever had someone say to you, "You can do anything you want to do with your life?" I know parents and teachers are well–intentioned when they encourage us this way. But, our natural bent will have something to say about what we can and can't accomplish.

For example, as a young boy, I began taking piano lessons. Over time, I was able to grasp the concept of scales and even became pretty proficient at playing the notes. But I couldn't really make the music. My piano playing was just so much plinking of keys on a keyboard. The inclination to excel just wasn't there, either, especially once I realized I had to practice so much. I was more interested in playing baseball or football with my friends. In this case, I had some ability, but no real interest.

On the other hand, I mentioned earlier my desire (dream?) to be a professional golfer. I was passionate about the game, even enrolling for a class during my first semester in college. For weeks, we practiced hitting golf–ball sized Wiffle balls. You really can't be more serious than that about the game of golf! But, no matter how much I practiced, I had to accept the fact that I would be nothing more than an average golfer. Realizing that dampened some of my passion for golf as a profession. This time, I did have the interest, but not enough ability.

My experience represents the first piece in the puzzle that is our NICHE, identifying our skills, or natural bent. Our natural bent represents the intersection of our abilities (skills we are able to perform fairly well) and our interests (activities and areas of life that hold a strong attraction and enjoyment). It isn't enough just to have ability <u>or</u> interest; our natural bent encompasses both.

How would you describe your natural bent? What skills and abilities would you identify? Finish this sentence: *Something I've been told I'm good at is* ...... (To get you thinking about possibilities, take a look at the "Skills and Interests Categories" in Appendix One.)

Even as I ask you to consider that question, I can hear some insisting, "But I don't really have any skills." You see, we're quick to acknowledge the skills of others, especially those of artists or athletes. But, we're seemingly too "humble" to concede that we might have skills, too. We may not be aware of our skills or we may not consider how significant they really are or can be. But, God has created all of us with the skills necessary for survival. As well, he has gifted us with abilities that allow us to serve him and others, to make our life more purposeful and enjoyable. *Give God some credit*!

My friend, Bo Prosser, is Coordinator of Organizational Relationships for Cooperative Baptist Fellowship. Bo tells the story of a lady whose natural bent was hairdressing. She just loved to care for and style ladies hair—and she was good at it. But, how do you use a skill like hairdressing to serve God and others?

She shared her natural bent with her pastor who was just as perplexed about how she could use her skill. Later that day, while driving home, her pastor passed a senior adult home. Suddenly, the light went on. "Who would appreciate more the opportunity to talk with someone while having their hair done than the women who live there?" With that, a ministry of hairdressing was born.

Similarly, God creates all of us with potential. That's especially true where natural bent is concerned. What we do with that potential and whether or not we choose to develop it is totally up to us. But,

if we choose not to grow our natural bent, we shouldn't blame God for our own shortcomings.

Strengths vs. Weaknesses

Beyond simply identifying our skill or lack of skill in certain areas, there is another question we need to consider related to our natural bent. That is, would you advise a person to focus on developing their strengths or improving their weaknesses? For example, would you have encouraged me to continue working on my golf game in spite of my seeming lack of necessary ability?

Another myth often maintained by well–meaning parents, educators, and others is that we strive to become a "well–rounded person", knowledgeable and capable in a variety of pursuits. That's not to suggest that we shouldn't attempt new activities or experiences. One of the worst things we can do is to continue to insist, "Someday I'm going to try that," only to look back later with regret and wonder why we never got around to actually doing so. In taking those risks, it's possible we'll discover abilities and interests we never knew we had.

But here's the dilemma we may, eventually, encounter. We may be open to pursuing a new vocation or hobby and even put forth great effort to become competent. But, at some point, we may realize we have limited ability we'll likely never be able to overcome, regardless of the hard work or practice we put in. When confronted with that reality, we may be tempted to compare ourselves with others and question why God didn't grant us that particular ability. We allow ourselves to feel guilty and inadequate, overlooking the natural bent with which God DID gift us.

Truth is, we tend to spend a lot of time and energy fretting about our weaknesses and what we're not able to do. By contrast, it's far healthier and more productive for us to focus *the majority of our effort* on the things we already do well. That's not to suggest that we stop

striving to become reasonably adept in an area of weakness. But, the wiser strategy of growing our already God–given strengths allows us to more effectively invest our potential in others while realizing personal fulfillment and meaning.

Let's be honest, though. Not always can we devote ourselves only to areas of strength. There are times in any role or job when we won't be able to avoid "paying the rent". That is, we'll be required to step out of our comfort zone and contribute in a way that we would acknowledge is, basically, outside our natural bent. For example, as a minister, I'll be the first to admit that I'm not so competent or comfortable doing funerals or making hospital visits. That's not to say that God hasn't stretched me through the years and given me the privilege (responsibility!) of those ministries. I can do both, but I go in feeling anxiety and come away feeling drained. I feel like I've been out on a ledge and need to retreat to my strengths.

So, don't hear me suggesting we never give attention to our weaknesses, especially when we see the possibility of some minimal improvement. I've worked HARD to develop skills needed for funerals and hospital visits. That's part of my role as a minister. But, in some ways, that area of ministry is like my golf game. No matter how much I practice and play, it's only going to get so much better.

Still, there are at least three areas of "weakness" to which all of us simply *must* devote time and attention.

1. Simply insisting, "Well that's just who I am" is no explanation at all for unchristian personal character. Wisdom requires that we do our best to root out those negative traits that hold us back.

2. Related to character is our attitude toward life and others. All of us know persons who seem convinced they have just been dealt a bad hand in life and they can do nothing to change their circumstances. Reality is, all of us have a choice about our outlook. For example, are you a jar is half–full or half–empty kind of person? Any of us have our own unique

and less than ideal circumstances to overcome. But, the choice is ours! Author and pastor Chuck Swindoll sums it up well:

> The longer I live, the more I realize the impact of attitude on life. Attitude, to me, is more important than education, than money, than circumstances, than failures, than successes, than what other people think or say or do. It is more important than appearance, giftedness or scale. It will make or break a company... a church... a home. The remarkable thing is we have a choice every day regarding the attitude we embrace for that day. We cannot change our past.... We cannot change the fact that people act in a certain way. We cannot change the inevitable. The only thing we can do is play on the one string we have, and that is our attitude.... I am convinced that life is ten percent what happens to me and ninety percent how I react to it, and so it is with you.... We are in charge of our attitudes.

3. How well do we relate to others? In his book, *48 Days to the Work You Love*, author and career coach Dan Miller has noted that 85% of our success is directly related to attitude, enthusiasm, self-discipline, and interpersonal expertise. Only 15% of the time do technical skills and educational credentials get us ahead. That being said, we can—and must—continually develop our people skills.

In the end, the greater return on our investment of time and energy will be spent developing strengths, instead of weaknesses. We need to get better at what we're already good at! The real potential of

our life's contribution is realized when we work to develop and serve through our God–given strengths, our natural bent.

So, put me in a teaching situation or a vision casting session. Give me the opportunity to plan an event or encourage a discouraged leader and I'm serving more in my "sweet spot." Those are the things that really light my fire! That's not bragging; that's just acknowledging who God created me to be and giving him the credit.

None of us are gifted or called to do everything well. Nowhere in Scripture are we told we're responsible for a natural bent we don't have. Build on strengths. We need to focus on who we already are rather than struggling to be someone we're not and never will be. As I discovered in the midst of my journey, that's a sure recipe for burnout. The real aspiration is to find ways to spend more of our time and energy doing the things we're actually gifted for and called to do. That's when we hit our stride and realize the genuine joy we seek.

Some may choose to disagree with me at this point. But, I see nothing selfish in avoiding, as much as possible, the drudgery, frustration, and anxiety of attempting to work out of weaknesses when we can be energized through our strengths. Granted, no job is perfect and we'll, likely, find ourselves paying that rent referred to earlier in order to keep any job. Assuming nothing can be done to adjust that role and we're unwilling to make a career change, my best advice is to find a hobby or avocation that engages our strengths away from the job.

Just because were busy doesn't mean we're productive or effective. The real return on our life's investment is realized when we work through our God–given strengths. Cartoonist Charles Schulz stated, "Life is a ten–speed bike. Most of us have gears we never use." The trick is to discover the "gears on our bicycle". The wise person will ask the question, *"What are the two or three things I do that are most valuable in my service for God and others?"*

P.S. If you are a leader of others, give your folks permission to work out of their natural bent, too. Don't encourage mediocrity and

frustration by expecting others to do everything well. Allow them to take center stage with their strengths. At the same time, don't waste time and energy fretting that you can't do what God has gifted them to do. As we allow others to flourish where they are gifted, we will work out of our strengths while delegating our weaknesses. It works out nicely for all of us.

LIFE COACHING QUESTIONS

- *What do you consider your greatest strength(s)? Your greatest weakness(es)? Be honest with yourself and give God some credit.*
- *What have you been told you're good at by others? What seems to come easy for you while others may be challenged when they attempt the same thing?*
- *What do you enjoy doing? How do you make time and opportunity for those activities you're good at and enjoy most?*
- *What are some of the "pay the rent" activities in your life or career? What are some activities that you've had to admit may be more weakness than skill for you?*
- *If you knew you couldn't fail, what are some skills you'd like to further develop? When you consider your current weaknesses, where do you see the most possibility for improvement?*
- *If you make no changes in your current skill level, what will be the outcome? Whose fault will it be?*
- *When considering your natural bent and how you might develop it, what are your next practical steps for doing so?*

CHAPTER 4

I-NDIVIDUAL PERSONALITY

I have a longtime acquaintance who is one of the most outgoing individuals I've ever met. C.W. is the kind of guy who never meets a stranger. Not only is he outgoing, but he's passionate, too —— passionate about introducing others to Jesus. I've often joked with others that C.W. would think nothing of walking into a bar and initiating a spiritual conversation.

For a long time, it bothered me that I couldn't be more like C.W. I sought training to be more outgoing and effective in sharing Christ with others. I tried my best to be as gregarious as C.W. But, after a while, I accepted the fact that's just not who I was.

Then, an even more sinister thought entered my mind. If I can't be like C.W., can God use me at all? Here I am called to ministry and I have an introverted personality! It really bothered me for a long time. Over time, I came to realize that C.W. and others with a unique personality like him weren't the only persons God could use. I ceased comparing myself to him and determined it was okay to simply be who God created me to be. C.W. had his own unique personality and I had mine. One wasn't better than the other. We were just different!

Like no two snowflakes are alike, God gave us a personality unlike any other person's personality. Then, get this — God threw

away the mold! It's truer than we realize: Each of us really do march to the beat of a different drummer

Typically, when we hear the word "personality", we picture a person's appeal or likeable disposition. There's an attractiveness about them that makes them pleasant to be around. But personality is more than that. Personality describes what comes naturally to us or makes us totally uncomfortable in a given situation. Seen another way, personality is that combination of our God–given preferences for how we respond to situations in life. Further ingrained by upbringing, life circumstances, past experiences, etc., personality colors:

- how we relate to others
- how we take in and process necessary information for making decisions
- our response to problem situations
- how we approach tasks in life

Here's Looking at You!

Using personality types identified by the Myers–Briggs Personality test, we can gain some insight into our own personality preferences using the following scales and summaries. Then, with these summary statements in mind, consider some questions that may help us zero in on our preferred personality type.

Just remember, these summaries represent generalizations that may not *always* apply to specific individuals or to every specific situation in which we find ourselves. Though we tend to lean more toward one or the other personality types, all of us will have a little bit of all types in us. And avoid the tendency to view one personality type as better than another. That's not the case; they're just unique.

INTROVERT   EXTROVERT

Introversion vs. Extroversion expresses our preference for focusing on our inner world (ideas) or the outside world (other people).

When people hear the word, "introvert", they tend to picture a shy, maybe even antisocial person. Speaking as one, though, I enjoy people and feel comfortable in most social settings. It's just that, in time, those situations drain me. I need some "time out" to recharge. Extroverts, on the other hand, recharge their batteries among people. If they're by themselves for too long, they actually lose energy.

An introvert, will prefer working alone, one–on–one, or behind the scenes. They are usually quiet and reserved, comfortable reflecting on their own thoughts and ideas. Only after having carefully thought through their ideas will they risk sharing them with others. Introverts tend to prefer fewer close friends.

By contrast, the extrovert is more comfortable "out front", preferring groups and activity. Outgoing and usually more talkative, they enjoy interacting and are eager to share their thoughts with others. Extroverts tend to talk while they think; in a sense, they're thinking out loud. In general, extroverts consider anybody on Facebook a potential friend.

Which phrases most describe how you relate to your world?

INTROVERT	EXTROVERT
Inwardly focused; thoughtful	*Outwardly focused; gregarious*
Enjoy people—to a point!	*Enjoy people—all the time!*
Comfortable being alone	*Comfortable with other people*
Recharge by time alone	*Recharge with others*
Prefer one–on–one situations	*At home in crowds*
Quieter; reserved	*Outgoing; more talkative*
May prefer to work alone	*May prefer to work with a team*

- *Are you a people person (Extrovert) or do you tend to spend more time with your inner self and thoughts (Introvert)?*

- *Do you enjoy people anytime, anywhere (Extrovert) or do you enjoy being around others, but only for a limited duration (Introvert)?*

- *Are you energized by being around people (Extrovert)? Or do you prefer to recharge your batteries with time alone (Introvert)?*

- *Do you prefer group activities (Extrovert) or more solitary activities such as reading or involvement in a hobby (Introvert)?*

- *Do you feel more comfortable in crowds (Extrovert) or prefer time spent with a very few close friends (Introvert)? Do you prefer a quiet environment (Introvert) or more of an ongoing hubbub (Extrovert)?*

- *Do you prefer to take the lead (Extrovert) or are you more comfortable, more often than not, allowing others to take charge (Introvert)?*

- *Are you eager to share your thoughts and ideas with others (Extrovert)? Or, are you more cautious about when and how to share your deepest thoughts (Introvert)?*

SENSING   INTUITION

Sensing vs. Intuition refers to how persons process available data and view the world around them.

Sensors, as the word suggests, process information and take in their surroundings through their senses. Common sense and practicality are watchwords for them. They are comfortable in the "real world" with its facts, details, and routine. Sensors live in the here–and–now. More often, they prefer careful assessment before attempting to alter the status quo. They view life as a step–by–step progression.

By contrast, Intuitives process data on the basis of hunches, insights, and theory. Where the sensor is more concrete in their thinking, the intuitive is an abstract thinker. They are thoroughly

at home with novelty and new approaches to routine problems or situations. Theirs is an "ideal world", focused on a bigger picture and dreaming of what could be rather than what already is. Life for them is more about the journey to be enjoyed along the way rather than a perceived destination.

Which phrases most describe how you process information?

SENSOR	INTUITIVE
Realistic	*Idealistic*
More comfortable with facts	*More comfortable with ideas*
Generally prefer same–	*Generally prefer change*
old, same–old	*and challenge*
Focus on "what already is"	*Focus on "what could be"*
How do we do this?	*We can do this!*
We've always done it this way	*Let's try a new approach*
Routine	*Novelty*
Details	*Big picture*
Planner	*Make it up as you go along*
Tell time by a clock	*It feels like lunchtime*

- *Do you prefer "just the facts" (Sensor) or do you lean toward the pursuit of novel concepts and ideas (Intuitive)?*
- *Are you comfortable with what already exists and the way things always have been (Sensor) or are you open to new possibilities, tending to ask "What if ..." (Intuitive)? Would you prefer to build a new and improved mousetrap (Intuitive) or make the old mousetrap work better (Sensor)?*
- *Would you consider yourself to be a down to earth person recognized by others for your common sense (Sensor)? Or are you more of an idealist and a dreamer (Intuitive)?*
- *When presented with a new idea, would you typically respond, "We'll find a way to make this work?" (Intuitive) Or, is your*

> *first thought, "I don't really see how we can make this work?"*
> *(Sensor)*

- *Are you a details person (Sensor) or do you tend to see the big picture (Intuitive)? Do you tend to see the trees (Sensor) or the forest (Intuitive)?*
- *Do you prefer a step–by–step plan (Sensor)? Or, are you okay with improvising and playing it by ear (Intuitive)?*
- *Are you one who relies on your watch for the time of day (Sensor)? Or, would you rely more on a "sixth sense" to judge the time of day?" (Intuitive)*

THINKING   FEELING

Thinking vs. feeling describes how persons make needed decisions.

Thinkers are objective, prone to analysis of a situation or problem. Logic and reasoning are keys for decision–making. Though not totally oblivious to the value of relationships, their real priority is accomplishment of the task at hand or the destination to be gained.

In some ways, feelers may be just as rational and task–oriented as Thinkers. But personal values and needs of others are considerations in any decision. They tend to make decisions with their heart more than their head. For them, the people they work with and whether or not their work reflects their personal values will be as important as the assigned task.

Which phrases most describe you when making decisions?

THINKER	FEELER
More logical and objective	*More driven by emotion and empathy*
Relies on policies/procedures in decision–making	*Concerned about impact of decisions on persons*
Tends to view situations in black and white	*Sees more of the "gray" in a situation*

Pros vs. cons *People and feelings*
Task–oriented *People–oriented*
Tell the truth; put all the *Be tactful; avoid conflict*
cards on the table *when possible*
Decide based on your head *Decide based on your heart*
Logical, organized *"Gut feeling"*

- *In making a decision, would you tend to rely on the rule book and established procedures (Thinker)? Or, would you be more concerned about how a possible decision will impact the persons involved (Feeler)?*

- *Do you typically see only one clear solution to a problem situation (Thinker)? Or, would you be willing to consider that there may be more than one approach to solving a problem (Feeler)?*

- *Do you tend to use a pros vs. cons list in deciding (Thinker)? Or, are you at least as concerned for the persons impacted by the decision (Feeler)?*

- *Is your primary consideration accomplishment of the required task (Thinker) or does concern for others guide, at all, your approach to the task (Feeler)?*

- *Which is more important: a considerate response (Feeler) or the cold, hard facts (Thinker)?*

- *Would you tend to avoid conflict for the sake of harmony (Feeler)? Or, would you think it's best to clearly state your position and let the cards fall where they may (Thinker)?*

- *Do you make decisions based on "gut feelings" (Feeler) or are you more logical, more organized (Thinker)?*

JUDGING   *PERCEIVING*

Judgers vs. perceivers offers insight in to how you order your world and live your observable life with others.

Judgers are planners; they prefer to plan their work and work their plan. They're more comfortable with organization, systems,

and predictability. Calendars, schedules, and to–do lists are indispensable tools for them to make it through their day. To finish a task or achieve closure on a problem is the objective.

Perceivers are more spontaneous, tending to go with the flow. They will tolerate a Judger, but feel handcuffed by their preferences. They aren't at all flustered by new information that may require a last–minute adjustment.

Which phrases best describe how you interact with your world?

JUDGER	**PERCEIVER**
Seek closure	*Can live with open–ended*
Planner	*Adapter*
Make a decision!	*We need more information!*
Results	*Process*
To–do list and schedule	*Go with the flow*
Neat, well–organized	*Okay with clutter*
Agenda	*What agenda?*
Time conscious; punctual	*More spontaneous and flexible*
There's one right way to do this!	*There's more than one way to do this!*
One task at a time	*Multitasking*

- *Do you prefer decisiveness and closure (Judger) or do you tend to keep your options open before making a decision (Perceiver)?*
- *Are you one who lives by structure — plans, calendars, schedules, and to–do lists (Judger)? Or, do you prefer being more spontaneous, even changing course in the middle of the stream (Perceiver)?*
- *Is there typically one right way to do something (Judger)? Or, are you open to more than one way or even someone else's approach to accomplishing a task (Perceiver)?*
- *Are you concerned that your desk is neat and organized (Judger)? Or, are you content to function with "order amid chaos" (Perceiver)?*

Even as we respond to these questions, there are three implications we need to keep in mind as we explore the ranges of personality.

1. When it comes to personality, we are not either/or all the time. In any given situation, we may resort to a response that is totally opposite of our normal and preferred personality. For example, we may be an extrovert and usually enjoy the company of others. But that doesn't mean we may not choose some occasions to "retreat" and be by ourselves. But to do this too often creates awkwardness for us. It's like attempting to write with the wrong hand; we can do it, but it's not natural for us.

    In fact, if we consistently act contrary to our natural personality, we will find ourselves becoming discouraged, frustrated, and out of sync with the real us. Personality just means that, *in most instances*, we resort to a favorite way of responding to life situations.

2. God didn't make a mistake in creating any of us with a particular personality. There is no "best" personality. That we were created with a variety of personality means nothing more than we're wired differently! For example, though Thinkers may be more logical in their decision making, that doesn't mean they're totally uncaring of others. Nor does it mean a Feeler will simply throw logic to the wind. They just tend to focus more on the people side of the issue.

    We tend to focus on the negatives of our personality, rather than the possibilities. For example, because I prefer not to be out front too often, I've always wondered if my personality is an obstacle to leadership. But, amazingly, God continues to open doors for me and use me! Over time, I've come to understand that a lot happens behind the scenes. No one even knows the star has taken the stage until someone pulls the curtain! There are no inferior personalities and

there's no reason for any of us to feel guilty or apologize for who we are.

3. At the same time, God's Spirit can stretch our personality beyond our comfort zones to make us more useful and more comfortable in serving him and others. Early in our marriage, it made all the sense in the world for me to insist to Janie, "Well, that's just who I am. That's the way God made me." Needless to say, I wasn't off the hook with Janie. And, God won't accept that excuse from us, either.

The point is, our personality can be grown and stretched if we allow God's Spirit at work in us. Though I'm still an introvert at heart, I have found, over time, I'm becoming more comfortable with people. I may never move totally to the extroversion end of the scale and that may not be what God has in mind, anyway. But how can I respond to God's commission to love others if I opt for a hermit–like existence? Instead, because of my conviction that the relational side of us is critical, God is cultivating that side of me, too.

LIFE COACHING QUESTIONS

- *As you delved in to this element of your NICHE, you probably found yourself in more than one personality type. But, in general, if asked to describe my personality, I would say I am...*
- *How do you see your discoveries around your personality shaping your future life's path?*

CHAPTER 5

C-HARISMA (SPIRITUAL GIFTS)

Because I'm an avid college football fan, I sometimes enjoy asking this question in workshops just to make a point. "Who is the most important person on a football team?" Typically, the quarterback gets a lot of the credit. But, he's able to do nothing without blockers. He really can't even get the play started if someone doesn't, first, snap him the ball. In fact, what if somebody doesn't bother to put air in the ball?

I use that analogy to highlight the role and importance of spiritual gifts. Just as with the football team, each person with each spiritual gift has a significant role to play. The word "charisma", as we normally use it, refers to how we're drawn to an individual by their charm or appearance. But "charisma" is a good Biblical word, too, used to describe the spiritual giftedness of Christians. Spiritual gifts are a large part of the answer to the question, "What is my NICHE? What should I do with the one life God has given me?"

What Are Spiritual Gifts?

Spiritual gifts are supernatural abilities given by God to Christians at the moment of conversion to enable them to better serve him and others. Scripture tells us that when we receive Christ as Lord and Savior, his

Holy Spirit comes to live within us (Acts 2:38). At that moment of spiritual rebirth, we were "gifted" with one or more spiritual abilities. Our spiritual gifts may well complement our other skills, interests, and personality. We didn't earn them or acquire them. But, God graciously gives them to us only because he wants our lives to be useful for him and meaningful for us. In every sense of the word, they are "grace gifts".

By gifting us, we're able to do for God things that can be explained only one way — he's at work in us! For example, one Christian may have the gift of teaching. It's a gift that represents one way they most enjoy serving God. That doesn't necessarily mean they're the most accomplished teacher you'll ever meet. After years of teaching, they still get "butterflies in their stomach" when they stand before their students. Part of that is recognition of the awesome responsibility and privilege of a teacher. But, they realize their teaching ability, even after all the "practice" they've had, remains limited. Even so, God seems to use them to communicate his Word to others. There are times they're able to share an insight, knowing that insight isn't their own. That is truly supernatural!

The gifts of the Spirit are varied and different. In Scripture, we find what appear to be *representative* lists of gifts (See 1 Corinthians 12, Romans 12, and Ephesians 4). Though some may disagree, I'm convinced these lists are not exhaustive at all in describing the gifts God provides for us. For example, how many times have we found ourselves in the presence of God when a person sings or plays an instrument? Others do the same thing through their writing. What many might consider little more than a talent is used to connect persons with God.

Below is a list and brief description of some spiritual gifts most commonly exercised by Christians:

- **Evangelism**
    a. A deep sense of the spiritual lostness of persons.
    b. Deep desire, boldness, and unique capacity to share the gospel effectively.

    c. Are continually seeking to initiate conversation with those who are spiritually lost. (E.g., my friend C.W.)

- **Teaching**
  - a. The ability to grasp and communicate Bible truths so that others may understand and see the relevance of God's Word to life.
  - b. Most often, but not always, expressed in the local church context.
- **Faith**
  - a. One who is able to believe God for what seems impossible.
  - b. Characteristic of the "prayer warrior" who is able to pray often and with perseverance for the physical and spiritual needs of others.
- **Leadership**
  - a. Able to discern God's vision and purpose for a group of believers, to develop goals and strategies as a means of accomplishing that vision, and able to motivate others toward those goals.
  - b. A gift exercised through serving others, not domination.
- **Administration**
  - a. The ability to guide and lead a church or group of believers to achieve their mission in an effective and organized manner.
  - b. Especially involves coordination of people/financial/physical resources.
- **Giving**
  - a. A willingness to give or part with personal possessions in order to further Kingdom advance.
  - b. May involve sacrificially giving money, time, or talent to the Lord's work.

- **Mercy**
  a. Christian compassion and empathy for those in dire need or crisis.
  b. The ability to recognize needs and *the willingness to go the extra mile to meet those needs.*
  c. Needs may include food, shelter, clothing, jobs, or simply personal attention.

- **Serving**
  a. The unique ability to recognize practical needs and joyfully help to meet those needs.
  b. Enjoy providing behind–the–scenes assistance to complement the overall ministry of the Church.
  c. Is the *diakonia* from which we get the word "deacon".

- **Hospitality**
  a. Able to make believers or strangers feel a part of the "family of God".
  b. May involve lodging, food, or fellowship in a home or church setting. (1 Peter 4:9)

- **Prophecy**
  a. The ability to declare a word from God in our world today.
  b. Though there may be an element of foretelling in the message, largely the message is one of God's work in our situation today.
  c. The "preaching" gift.

- **Exhortation**
  a. The ability to comfort and encourage others.
  b. Includes counsel that helps another reach their full potential.
  c. Note: There is a gift of encouragement, but no corresponding gift of discouragement. Wonder why some tend to practice the gift of discouragement, though?

- **Apostleship**
  - a. The ability to overcome barriers of culture, language, nationality, race, etc. in order to share the gospel.
  - b. The "missionary gift".

Why Does God Give Us Spiritual Gifts?

God saved us for more than eternity and heaven. He has a message he wants to communicate through us to a broken, needy, and hurting world. Our spiritual gifts are just one of the means for communicating that message.

Often our gifts will be used in our role as servant leaders within the church. For example, in Bible teaching or serving on a church committee, we may employ one or more spiritual gifts. But our gifts can be used (and should be!) just as readily beyond the church building. God doesn't limit himself to working inside the walls of a church only on Sundays. He's very much at work in our homes, workplaces, schools, and even the fringes of our communities — if we're looking for him. God can use our gifts to influence our neighbors, co-workers, and families if we're open to that possibility.

In fact, Christians are never more the Church than when we represent Christ in our homes and communities. We're naïve to believe God's Kingdom will advance if we can simply get enough people together in our churches on Sundays. That simply not going to happen! We have to be willing to utilize our spiritual giftedness on the "front lines" of our communities. What happens on Sunday inside the church building is important. But the real work of the Church is done "out there".

Not everybody is called to professional ministry. But every Christian is called to be a "minister" in their relationships of life. The call to salvation and the call to ministry are one and the same. The Biblical understanding of effective ministry is that all of us do it together, complimenting each other. God is calling each of us to

represent him right there in our business, in the school where we teach, on a construction site, or wherever our work takes us.

Truth is, the world each of us live in is exclusively ours. It is an absolutely awesome thought that each of us was uniquely created for this particular time in all of human history, to live in our "corner of the world", and with our particular spiritual gifts, relationships, and opportunities to serve God and others. Out of all the billions of people who have walked this earth to this point and in the future, none has had a "heartbeat" exactly like ours." If we don't exercise our spiritual giftedness in "our world", who will?

The Parable of the Talents (Matthew 25:14–30) is not just about financial resources. It's about potential and opportunities, too. God is looking for those who will be faithful with a few things in order to be given opportunity to do even greater things. In my mind, failure to become the best I can be represents personal failure and sin. How it must pain our Creator God to see us forfeit our potential on a false altar of "good enough". How can I ever offer a God who gave his best an attitude of just good enough?

But I Don't Have a Spiritual Gift!

Au contraire! If you're a Christian, you certainly do have at least one spiritual gift and likely more! There's no real humility in insisting you don't. We may not know what our gift is right now, but it's a blatant denial of Scripture to argue we have no spiritual gift. Paul reminds us, "Now to each one the manifestation of the Spirit is given for the common good." (1 Corinthians 12:7). If we are truly a believer in the Biblical sense, we can safely conclude we have one or more spiritual gifts.

Our spiritual gifts probably don't come to us anywhere near fully developed. With arrival of our gifts begins a life–long process of cultivating them for further use. The gifts God graciously provides may well complement our already existing abilities and skills. In that

sense, we may already have a head start on developing a particular gift and its use.

By the way, how do we distinguish between talents and spiritual gifts? Just to be clear, both talents and spiritual gifts are from God. But, talents are given at birth, not at conversion. Even unbelievers have natural talents. In fact, our spiritual gifts may serve to further compliment the talents we already possess. Both talents and spiritual gifts should be and can be used to serve God and others. But, the distinction can be quickly made by looking at the motivation behind the use of talents and spiritual gifts. If the motivation is to honor God and point others to him, then we can be sure spiritual giftedness is at work.

How Do I Discover My Spiritual Gifts?

There are several approaches to take in identifying the gift(s) we possess. I would suggest a combination of any and all of these steps.

- **Pray**, asking God to point you in the direction of your spiritual giftedness. I know prayer is always a safe "Sunday school" answer to a question about our spiritual life. But, rest assured, your spiritual gifts mix is not a classified secret to be known only by God. In fact, just the opposite. God is eager that you be aware of and confidently exercise your spiritual gifts. Otherwise, they simply lay dormant. Appendix Two includes a "Prayer Guide" for use in discovering your gifts.
- **Seek counsel from mature Christians** who've seen you in action. When have others witnessed you at your best in serving God and others? What words of affirmation and encouragement have you heard from others?
- Consider what you can learn from **spiritual gifts assessments**. There are a number of gifts assessments available, many for free on the Internet. Feel free to disagree,

but I'm not a raving fan of these instruments. That's not to say they're worthless. They certainly can be a *starting point* for assessing spiritual giftedness. But, I would caution you about allowing an assessment to become the final word about your gifts mix.

For one thing, in the past, we may have admired how God uses certain gifts with others. We yearn to be used similarly by God. So, we respond to the assessment in a way that "fixes" conclusions reached about our gift mix.

But the greater flaw with these assessments is we may "pigeonhole" ourselves, concluding we simply don't have a particular gift. That is, based on an assessment completed in the past, a person may insist they simply don't have the gift of evangelism, teaching, hospitality, or whatever gift you choose. For example, I often use the facetious example of becoming involved in a conversation with a passenger in the seat next to me on a plane. When the conversation turns to spiritual matters, that's not the time to stand and inquire, "Is there someone on board with the spiritual gift of evangelism? I've taken this conversation about as far as I can go!"

Instead, God has placed that opportunity before me and, though I may not have the full measure of the spiritual gift of evangelism, I have been given enough to respond to my fellow passenger's questions. That I don't have as much understanding of the gift of evangelism doesn't release me from the opening before me right now. In fact, this may be the occasion God uses to further develop that seed of the evangelism gift in me.

- My best advice for discovering your spiritual gifts is **just do it!** Rather than waiting for God to reveal our gifts to us, why not just jump in feet first and attempt something for God? In time, we discover what we're best equipped for and the unique giftedness God crafted in us. As my former colleague

with Virginia Baptists, Bill Alphin, suggests, "Gifts 'bubble up' through experience."

My guess is that many Christians would confess they had no idea how their spiritual giftedness could provide such meaning and satisfaction until they found themselves in a situation requiring them to respond. For my part, that's how I discovered my spiritual gift for teaching. As a young minister just out of seminary, part of my role included a weekly Bible study with the youth. Though I, initially, felt thrust into the role and went in with fear and trembling, I soon discovered I enjoyed the preparation and interaction with the kids. A whole new avenue of service was opened for me.

How many spiritual gifts will we discover? Maybe some of all of them, though some may be more developed than others. But, as a Christ follower, we have been given at least enough giftedness to respond in those opportunities God provides.

What if I don't have the spiritual gift I really want most? Again, feel free to disagree with me. But, I suspect all of us have a mix that includes many or all of the spiritual gifts listed in Scripture. Some are primary for us, some more secondary. But, at some point, we must trust the One who created us to be able to provide us the satisfaction and meaning we really desire. We don't always know what's best for us!

Like others, I will confess I admire how God uses some individuals I know in unique ways. I've watched, for example, those with the gift of preaching. I marvel at how God uses them in such a natural and effective way to share his Word with others. The practical insights God shares through them simply astound me. How can I have read that passage so many times before and not see that implication?

Though I may long for that gift, I've accepted the fact that preaching simply isn't a primary part of my gift mix. At best, I'm an

adequate preacher. Going back to discovery of my gift for teaching. At the time, it was a gift I had never explored or even considered. But, seizing (or stumbling upon!) those opportunities given me, I discovered a whole new open door of meaning and fulfillment. A gift that made all the difference for me was lying practically dormant all the time.

Are some spiritual gifts more important than others? For some, there will be the temptation, based on their giftedness, to consider themselves spiritually superior to others. That's especially true if their gift is a high–profile and out front gift such as teaching or prophecy.

And, knowing our tendency to compare ourselves and our abilities to others, the more high profile gifts (e.g., preaching, teaching, evangelism, etc.) seem to draw a lot of our attention. But, all the gifts are important and have their place. In 1 Corinthians 12, Paul notes that, just as the parts of the human body are interdependent, so are the spiritual gifts God gives to the Church. Consider, for example, how some exercise the gift of service. Nobody really notices what those who serve behind the scenes do. But, let what they do go undone and everybody notices!

One word of caution as you seek to determine your spiritual gifts mix. Avoid the danger of "analysis paralysis". Keep in mind, any attempt to discover our spiritual gifts is not an exact science. That's okay. We're on a faith journey. That leaves open the possibility of a great deal of experimentation. But the point is not simply that we know what our spiritual gifts are; they are to be used!

When we do employ our spiritual gifts, at least three outcomes are inevitable:

1. We make a difference in our family, our community, and our "corner of the world"
2. We impact eternity through the generations who will follow us. That's our legacy.
3. One day we will hear from Jesus himself, "Well done, good and faithful servant."

LIFE COACHING QUESTIONS

- *God gifted me to _____.*
- *In serving God, I feel most comfortable and fulfilled when _____.*
- *What roles of leadership or kinds of service have I attempted in the past and received affirmation or encouragement from others, especially trusted Christian friends?*
- *What do I really enjoy doing for God? What have I attempted for God that seemed relatively easy for me? What have I attempted for God that gave me the most satisfaction? (In a sense, our spiritual gifts reflect a life's passion that must be lived out.)*
- *What roles of leadership or service have I attempted in the past that made me feel uncomfortable? (This question identifies areas where we may not be quite as gifted.)*
- *With proper training for a particular area of service, I can see myself _____.*
- *If I could really make a difference for Christ in our world, I'd like to do so by _____.*
- *If I could design or choose an area of service in which I would feel most comfortable, most fulfilled, and most used of God, it would be _____.*
- *What are your spiritual gifts? What have you discovered about your spiritual gifts mix? What have you discovered to be your primary spiritual gift?*
- *How comfortable do you feel responding to questions from others about your spiritual gifts?*

CHAPTER 6

H-EART AND PASSION

"We act as though comfort and luxury were the chief requirements of life, when all that we need to make us happy is something to be enthusiastic about."

— Charles Kingsley, professor, novelist, and priest of the Church of England

As a baseball fan growing up, I was fascinated by stats and records. One of those "records never to be broken" was former New York Yankee first baseman Lou Gehrig's streak of playing in 2,130 consecutive games. But then, starting on May 30, 1982, Cal Ripken, Jr., infielder for the Baltimore Orioles, began his own remarkable streak of consecutive games played.

Because I admired Ripken so much as both a person and a player, I will never forget the September night in 1995 when Cal broke Gehrig's record. While millions watched on television, he took a victory lap around Camden Yards to a standing ovation that lasted more than twenty two minutes. After that night, he would continue the streak, playing another 502 consecutive games before *he decided* it was time for the streak to end in September 1998.

Just think of it. For more than sixteen seasons, Ripken was dressed and ready to play every single game of a 162–game season.

Imagine the off–season conditioning he endured to prepare for season after season. Throw in all the batting practice and fielding practice he took. There were long plane rides and, as the streak grew, the same questions over and over from the media. Can we possibly imagine the minor injuries, the upset stomachs, headaches, and fatigue he played through during the streak? Night after night, day after day, at home and in cities on the road, he was always at his locker, ready to put on his Orioles uniform. What a routine! Don't you think there were days when he wished he could take a day off rather than play?

Later, Ripken would state, "If there was one thing that helped me break the record, I loved every second of what I did." That's the power of passion.

Is Pursuit of My Passion Self–Serving?

In the minds of some, living for God and serving others means we must sacrifice our own meaning and fulfillment. Practically speaking, they would have us believe discovering God's will is to determine what we most want to do — and then do just the opposite! In their view, anyone who would pursue the joy of living out of their passion is flirting with sin. Life in Christ is about suffering, sacrifice, self–effacement — well, you get the picture.

Still others would argue that pursuing our passion is, at its core, self–serving. They insist we should shove our passion into the background and get on with making a life in the real world. No doubt, our passion for just about anything can cross the line and become all–consuming and self–absorbing. We can find ourselves neglecting family and other key relationships.

But, God isn't asking us to sacrifice our enthusiasm for life in order that we serve him and others. Where in Scripture does God ever say we can't or shouldn't wholeheartedly enjoy life, just going through the motions of our earthly existence? God created us for

that kind of meaning and fulfillment that will draw others to him. For goodness sakes, he is the author of abundant life! Now, as we've seen, whether we access that offer is up to us.

In his book, *Start With Why*, author Simon Sinek is, primarily, speaking to organizations and businesses. But, much of the wisdom he offers applies to individuals, too. According to Sinek, most of us know *what* we do to make a life for ourselves and *how* we go about doing so. But, not so many of us give thought to or can articulate WHY we live life as we do. What's your purpose, your cause in life? And why should you or anyone else care?

The world falsely promises that money and more of it is the answer to all our deepest needs. Even as millions pursue the myth, they're discovering the lie in that. We need a cause beyond amassing wealth or simply making a living. Pursuit of wealth can never be the be–all and end–all point of life. At best, money is little more than a tool that allows us to seek our real God–ordained purpose in life, that of investing in others. That's why so many today are opting out of the "rat race" and entering a second career more focused on helping others.

Theologian Frederick Buechner so aptly stated, "The place God calls you to is the place where your deep gladness and the world's deep hunger meet." Realistically speaking, it's not hard at all to spot the great pockets of need that exist in our world. The real difficulty is the effort required to discover my great passion in response to that need instead of just going through the motions of life, oblivious to a hurting world around me. To do so, though, opens the door to serving God and others even as we experience the meaning and fulfillment we've been seeking all along.

Is it possible when we discover that cause, that passion that makes a difference in our world, we uncover that purpose for which we were created? As Bill Hybels, pastor of Willow Creek Community Church near Chicago, puts it, our passion is about discerning our "white hot why". God has hard–wired in each of us the aspiration for making a difference in our world, to have our life count for more

than self–serving pursuits. To discover real need in our world (not mere busywork, but service that really makes a difference) and to simply *ache* to spend ourselves in meeting that need is the essence of joy and passion.

Let me be quick to state, I'm not naive enough to insist that everything I do in ministry entails that level of passion for me. There are, in fact, times when any Christian leader will feel overworked, undercompensated, and, generally, taken for granted and unappreciated. But, to be able to respond to God's call, the world's need, and my need all at the same time — does it get any better than that?

Live IN To Your Passion

We've all heard, "Do what you love and you'll never work a day in your life." Passion transforms even work into a form of play! That's not to suggest living in to our passion allows us to never do a real day's work the rest of your life. Doing so may require a lot of courage and determination. We may find ourselves swimming upstream against the expectations of others or even the expectations we've always had for ourselves.

Ardently pursuing our passion will require LOTS of hard work. For one thing, because we are passionate about something means we want to do it with excellence. As an example, we could all name actors or actresses whose passion for their craft comes through on the screen. What we don't see is the training and rehearsals that go on behind the scenes. We don't see the years of heartbreak and rejections. We never get an inside look at the discipline and determination to rise above that.

Pursuing our passion is about uncovering the real us and why we exist at all. But, living in to our passion may not allow us an impulsive decision to walk away from our day job. For example, in his book, *Simplify*, Bill Hybels chronicles John Grisham's transition

from an attorney who hated his job to chasing his dream of being a best–selling novelist. It all started innocently enough as Grisham challenged himself to write just one page a day. Over time, those pages added up. In the meantime, continuing to practice law paid the bills.

Still, it's my conviction that all of us should seek to spend our life doing something we love to do. We seem drawn to the possibility that our life could be about more than simply making a living and surviving one more day. With all my heart, I'm convinced God created us to thrive! If having difficulty determining your God–given purpose, start by taking a look at your passion. That will, almost inevitably, lead you to your purpose. God is granting you permission to experiment a little. Enjoy!

The Bible is filled with the accounts of persons with passion. For example, Paul's passion early in life, misguided as it was, included ridding the world of Christians. After his Damascus Road experience, his zeal focused on sharing Christ with that same world. Nehemiah's passion was for rebuilding a broken down city wall. David's passion was worship and praise of God. Solomon, passionately, searched for the meaning of life. In the case of each, pursuit of that passion resulted in them and their life never again being the same.

But, too many of us opt for what seems to be security and comfort rather than pursue our real life's calling and passion. In doing so, we find ourselves on an endless treadmill, wondering, "Is this all my life was meant to be?" It's my firm belief that we'll never know the real peace and security we seek, much less the meaning in life, when we buy into conventional wisdom about how persons should or shouldn't spend their life. The result is we find ourselves showing up at the same time every day to put in another boring day at a job we can't stand before heading home. After all, we rationalize, that's just the way life is; those are the cards I've been dealt. In the process, we've become untrue to ourselves and have failed the God who created us for so much more.

Remember as children how we dreamed of being a firefighter, an astronaut, a professional athlete, an artist, actress, or ballet dancer? The sky was the limit. What happened to those color–outside–the–lines dreams? It's true, our passion may have outpaced our ability to actually enter those professions (remember the earlier discussion of natural bent). But, in some cases, have we sacrificed our passion to become the "responsible and realistic" adult everyone expected us to be?

I happen to have a career in this season of my life that allows me to tap into two of my passions – teaching and writing. Away from the office, I'm able to enjoy other passions, for example, reading, watching college sports, and playing golf. Just getting on the course allows me to relax and stir those competitive juices I've always had.

I understand not everyone can enjoy their work life as much as I do. You may find yourself in a season of life or a stage of family life where making a living is a real priority. To be truthful, I've found myself there, too. Work can't always be fun. Still, your response to this question could be especially revealing: *If money were no object, would I still be going to the job I have now?*

But, if you can't change your life's work, at least change your life away from work. Find an avocation or hobby that really lights your fire. Just like Grisham, begin writing a page a day. Maybe you do have to endure the drudgery of a job that allows you to do little more than "pay the rent". But, that job then frees you up to spend time on pursuits that are more aligned with your passion. Meanwhile, are there steps (training, education, experience, etc.) you can be taking now to prepare to move into a vocation that incorporates more of your passion(s)?

You and I have one life and one life only we can offer this world. Living in to our passion represents good stewardship of life. Not only do we realize personal meaning and fulfillment, but I'm also convinced we perform better when passionate about whatever path our lives may take. And, that passion, whether pursued vocationally or as avocation, will keep us going in the hard times.

Live OUT of Your Passion, Too!

Remember, discovering your NICHE is not about you, alone. Yes, it's the life you were created for and a path to a life of contentment and fewer regrets. But, it's also the means for you to make a difference in your world. The truly lasting joy in life is found as we invest ourselves in others.

Only a cause worth giving ourselves to will find us jumping out of bed each morning rather than giving in to the temptation to pull the covers over our head. Sadly, too many of us view life as little more than a way to make a living and survive with some semblance of creature comfort. But when we come to the end of life, will it be enough for our epitaph to read, "He knew 'the good life' "? If you and I don't have a vision for leaving this world a better place and enthusiasm (passion!) for making it happen, I seriously question whether our life will amount to as much as it potentially could. Without question, it takes more than passion to make what could be and should be a reality. But, passion rekindles our resolve when confronted with the tough realities of life.

Consider the Biblical account of Esther, a young Jewish lady who had been adopted and raised by her cousin, Mordecai. Though Persian King Xerxes (485–464 B.C.) was unaware of her Jewish heritage, Esther had caught his eye and he made her his queen. In spite of her lofty position, Mordecai cautioned her to continue keeping her Jewish identity a secret.

Enter the villain in our story, a man named Haman. An Amalekite and sworn enemy of the Israelites, he was second only to the king in power. His position demanded other officials bow in honor to him. An ongoing feud erupted when, Mordecai, who had his own minor role in the king's administration, refused to compromise his religious convictions and bow to Haman.

Haman took advantage of this snub to hatch a plot to eliminate not only Mordecai but a campaign of genocide aimed at all Jews in the Kingdom. The king, convinced by Haman that a group of Jews

in the kingdom were not obeying Persian law, unwittingly issued a decree that all Jews should be killed.

Learning of the death sentence, Mordecai urged Esther to intercede with the king on behalf of her people. But there was great risk involved, even for the queen. If she approached the king uninvited, she could be executed. And, how would the king respond if he learned of her Jewish heritage? Mordecai, though, warned her that the decree could result in her death, too. In fact, he suggested to her, perhaps she had been given this unique opportunity to preserve the future of her people.

After a three–day fast, Esther approached the king. Seeing the king hold out his scepter, allowing her to enter, must have brought a sigh of relief. As the king learned of Haman's trumped up charges, he repealed his earlier decree and Haman was hanged on the very gallows he had built for execution of the Jews. Esther's passion for the future of her people overrode her fear and the risk of intruding on Persian policies

The Influence Our World Needs

> The waters of the Mississippi begin with a trickle in the upper Midwest. One seed can grow a forest. One candle can erase total darkness. Every journey starts with one small step. Similarly, every accomplishment starts with one small dream that is birthed by God's vision planted within an individual.

At some point, whether or not our life is making a difference will become an issue for most of us. A major issue! Like Esther, we'd like to believe our one solitary life will have significance. Will persons know, after we're gone, that we were here? But the world we live in today is so vast and the need is so great. Can one person really make a difference?

One look at today's headlines reminds us of the litany of issues we face. How do we make sense of a violent culture that leads children to ambush their schoolmates or fly airplanes into skyscrapers in order to further a religious and political agenda? What has created the vacuum of effective, moral leadership in our world? Or does it matter as long as we have our "peace and prosperity"? How do we counter the proliferation of perverse lifestyles and ideas imposed on us by those whose sole motivation is profit? Do we have no recourse for what is piped into our homes by cable television and the Internet? Have we become so bored and desensitized that we blindly fall at the altar of popular culture?

Spiritually, the family life of our nation is under attack. A concerted attempt is in the works to redefine the meaning of family. Adults living together outside marriage is one of the fastest growing living arrangements today, partially for tax reasons, but primarily because marriage is seen as a hindrance to personal fulfillment and independence. Many children have become "throwaways", left to fend for themselves. In our pursuit of the "good life", we insist on acquiring more things rather than investing time, energy, and resources in the future of children.

Ironically, it's possible to go an entire week in the workplace and never hear the name of God mentioned except in a profane or derogatory way. Yet, if we suggest that same God is the solution for our current social predicament, we're looked at as if we're aliens from another planet. We're seen as bigoted, imposing our own values on others!

Jesus made it plain to his disciples that the Christian worldview would never dominate our culture. He made it equally clear that we were not to adopt the ways of this world. Still, he left us here to be a godly influence. But too many of us have bought in to the mantra, "Don't impose your agenda on others". We are affected by culture more than culture is affected by us. What's to be done? What can anybody do to alter a culture already too far down the slippery slope?

Quite simply, Christians can make real inroads by our influence among those persons with whom we already live, do business, work, and play. Christians must become walking advertisements for meaningful life in Christ as an alternative to the confusion, boredom, and defeat that hounds the lives of so many. You and I may not be able to penetrate or influence all "worlds". But you and I can actually be "change agents" in our little corner of the world!

Even now, "ordinary" Christians are positioned in law, government, medicine, education, science, the arts, the media, sports, entertainment, business, and, of course, religion. Beyond those more public arenas, let's not forget the influence we can have in our own families and neighborhoods. Just think of the potential that already exists to share Christ's love, to influence and make a difference in the lives of individuals.

Martin Luther King once stated, "If a man hasn't discovered something he is willing to die for, he isn't fit to live." For what cause in life would we be willing to spend ourselves, as long as we live, even to the point of death? Will we have known more than just day–to–day existence and survival (which many assume is the essence of life) or have we given ourselves to something larger than us?

Those with passion care greatly about what God has called them to do. They find the energy and make the time for it. They will dream about, talk about, and enlist others to the cause that grips them. In short, people of passion make a difference in their world. If unwilling to live, *with passion*, the life of purpose God intended for us, we're likely to come to the end of life only to look back with a sense of regret.

A Word About Enlisting Other Leaders

Let me say a word to those charged with finding and enlisting leaders for their organization, specifically for the Church. Can a duck run? Sure, but not very well. For years, I have contended that

"we tend to enlist our own problems" when we ask persons to serve in leadership roles for which they are not really gifted or passionate. Then, we wonder why they don't flourish in their role. The goal is not to fill an organizational slot or even to enlist someone to do what you want done. The goal is to enlist someone who, like you, is passionate about the cause of Christ.

I sometimes have fun asking leaders this question: If you had to choose between competence or passion in enlisting a new leader, which would you choose? Almost always, they go with passion. After all, you can train for competence. Passion, not so easily.

What if we enlisted persons on the basis of their passion at least as much as their natural bent and spiritual gifts? What if we made persons aware of ministry opportunities and allowed them to respond based on their interest and enthusiasm for addressing that particular need? By doing so, we insure a motivated servant leader who is not serving simply because someone backed them into a corner. Rather, they really want to make a difference doing what they would love to do for God! Because of their enthusiasm, they're more likely to seek further training.

If you want to enlist effective, motivated leaders, give attention to matching their spiritual gifts and passion with ministry needs. More often than not, we enlist persons based on our organizational needs rather than their needs or the very real needs that exist in our communities. The result is their sense that what they do is little more than busywork.

I know you have slots to fill. But would I rather have an unfilled slot than a slot filled with someone not called to a particular ministry? Perhaps we even allow "migrating" to other leadership roles as persons experiment with those tasks that appeal to them.

Don't have enough leaders in your church or organization? Perhaps that's because persons are the victim of "arm twisting" that lands them in roles that are not a fit for who they are. Consider a way to walk persons through discovery of their NICHE, allowing

them to discover how gifted and talented they really are! Then, turn them loose to do what they do best!

LIFE COACHING QUESTIONS

- *I would love to _____.*
- *What one thing would I like to accomplish that would make a significant difference in my lifetime?*
- *What needs or causes really fire my imagination? What do I talk about and think about most?*
- *About what do I dream big dreams? What keeps me awake at night?*
- *What could I spend hours doing and never look at the clock once? Maybe not get paid!!*
- *If I could make a living at it, I would love to _____ for God.*
- *If I were to hit the lottery and suddenly making a living was no longer a question, how would I spend the rest of my life?*
- *For what cause am I eager to spend myself, perhaps even die? What is it that breaks my heart?*

CHAPTER 7

E-XPERIENCES AND ACCOMPLISHMENTS

"Experience is not what happens to a man. It is what a man does with what happens to him."
— Aldous Huxley, English writer and philosopher

"To each there comes in their lifetime a special moment when they are figuratively tapped on the shoulder and offered the chance to do a very special thing, unique to them and fitted to their talents. What a tragedy if that moment finds them unprepared or unqualified for that which could have been their finest hour."
— Winston Churchill, Prime Minister of the United Kingdom

There's one final piece to the puzzle that is our NICHE — we must take time to reflect on past experiences. We all have unique opportunities and relationships that have become such a part of who we are and continue to shape who we are. Because God never misses an opportunity to teach us and train us, we can be sure those experiences are key in understanding our NICHE. What lessons have we learned along the way?

One type of experience God is especially adept at using is crisis and suffering. That's not to suggest that those circumstances are necessarily God's will being orchestrated. It's simply to say that God will often use even the toughest circumstances in life to do his best work in us.

In my mid–thirties, I began experiencing pain in my upper legs. As a jogger and active in pick–up sports with my friends, it became a real aggravation. Eventually, after a series of medical tests, I was diagnosed with rheumatoid arthritis.

Initially, I assumed RA would mean just adjusting to ongoing aches and pains. But then, my doctors told me there would be no more running. That I would miss! Only later, did I realize the progressive and systemic nature of the disease, that it could attack other body organs. No, this was a life–changing experience.

Like many, I began to question God. "Why did this happen to me?" But, getting past the initial shock, God's teaching kicked in. My life priorities were reshaped. Key relationships in my life, especially with Janie, became more meaningful. Fewer things were taken for granted. I became more reliant on God just to get through the days. And, I discovered when you experience pain, it makes you more sensitive to the pain of others.

Along the way, I came to understand that I had not been targeted by God. I was just experiencing what it means for anyone, believer or otherwise, to live in a broken creation. I find reassurance in how career coach and author Dan Miller put it:

> "Sometimes we assume that our current situation reflects random, individual, disconnected events – or God maliciously making our life miserable. But none of those are likely true. Rather, we are where we are because each decision we make is a step in a particular direction. And over time that direction determines our position in our work, our finances, our health, our relationships and our spiritual well–being. If you think God did this to you,

then it justifies doing nothing until God changes your situation. And in doing nothing I see people open the door to blaming, resentment, anger, guilt and depression. I think God deserves better from us."

Before me lay a choice: Would I be a victim or a victor? It's one of life's great ironies that we have the ability to remember our past, but nothing we do can erase it. Oh, I missed the running and the way I felt before. But, it became clear to me that, if we continue to live in the past, it's because we choose to do so. We're children of God, not robots. A wiser stance is to consider what we can take from these past experiences that will enable us to better understand and accomplish God's purpose as we move into the future?

All of us face a similar choice, whether our experience goes back to childhood, school years, or some more recent event. Though natural to question "why" this happened to me, the more prudent step is to ask "what". That is, what can God teach me from this experience? Where does God want to take me from here? It may take some personal debriefing and some processing with trusted friends. But, regardless of what we're facing, God is not conspiring to bring us down.

Further, God isn't nearly so concerned with what has transpired in our life to this point. It's where we're willing to go with him from this point on that really makes the difference. For me, that's the essence of grace.

The Common Experience of Failure

As a ninth–grader in junior high school in Tallahassee, Florida, lightning struck and I won our school spelling bee. My prize was to represent our school at the county spelling bee. The big night arrived and there I stood at the microphone. My word to spell in the first round was "administer".

Now I knew how to spell that word. But I guess nerves took over and so I began, a–d–m–i–n–s–t–e–r, carelessly leaving out the second "i". The judge announced I had spelled the word incorrectly and I became the very first contestant to sit down. Worse than that, I had to look on, listening to others spell their words correctly while a county champion was crowned. All these years later, that one experience represents a memorable setback for me.

Past failures can be particularly haunting experiences for many of us. It won't take any of us long to recall a decision we made or a step that we took that didn't turn out just the way we had hoped. Then, when presented with a new opportunity, how Satan enjoys dredging up that setback from long ago to remind us we're not as smart or skilled as we may think we are. What makes us think this time would be any different? In a sense, a setback we suffered sometime in the past *has the potential* to defeat us once again.

Upfront, let's put all of our cards on the table. *Every single one* of us has similar experiences somewhere in our past. Even those who seem to have made it in life have failure in their background. In contrast to those who remain mired in past failures, though, they refused to be a victim of some long ago event or decision.

They've learned the distinction between a momentary setback and full–blown failure, too. To illustrate, picture a football running back. Handed the ball by his quarterback, he plunges into the line and moves the ball ahead five yards before being tackled. The failure is not that he was tackled; that's only a momentary setback. The real failure would be if he chooses not to get back up and take the ball the next time it's handed to him.

Similarly, we all experience setback in life. We made a bad decision or took a wrong step. It happens; welcome to the human race. But bad decisions or missteps don't make us a failure! Setbacks aren't fatal and our God is a God of second chances. None of us are throwaways from his point of view, in spite of the mistakes we may make along the way.

But, based on one temporary setback, many simply conclude, "I'm just destined to be a failure." That may be a convenient defense we lean on to excuse our decision not to get back in the game. But let's make a clear distinction between a circumstance in life — a momentary setback — and someone we aren't — a total failure. It's time we realize that none of us are failures because of past setbacks.

The distance between mere existence and a life of meaning and joy is measured, in part, by our response to momentary setback. The great early twentieth century sportswriter, Grantland Rice, compared the game of golf to life with all its stumbling blocks:

> "Because golf exposes the flaws of the human swing — a basically simple maneuver — it causes more self–torture than any game short of Russian Roulette. The quicker the average golfer can forget the shot he had dubbed or knocked off–line — and concentrate on the next shot — the sooner he begins to improve and enjoy golf. Like life, golf can be humbling. However, little good comes from brooding about mistakes we've made. The next shot, in golf or life, is the big one."

When we refuse to step through that next open door God presents to us, we move beyond setback to failure.

Just think of all the great experiences we would have missed if we hadn't tried and failed, then tried again! Unless we were exceptional, it's safe to assume we fell the first time we tried to walk. We probably floundered the first time we tried to swim. Were we able to ride our bicycle the first time we tried? Or hit a ball the first time we swung the bat? And think of all the lessons we would have missed along the way. In fact, wouldn't you agree that you've learned much more from your setbacks than you ever did from your successes? In a very real sense, you and I are, at least in part, the product of our setbacks and the lessons we learned from them. *But we are not a failure by virtue*

of who we are, our current circumstances, or any setbacks we may have experienced along the way.

Where we go from where we are now is what really counts. We can flirt with failure, choosing to whine and wallow in a past that was less than perfect. Or, we can grow beyond that past, accepting and even embracing the setbacks we've known. There are lessons to be learned. For one, we accept the fact that all our decisions will not be correct or perfect. Even so, our sovereign God is able to work through and around our mistakes. Our momentary setbacks may not be pleasurable and, certainly, there may be consequences to overcome. But, there are new decisions and new risks awaiting us out there. Will we allow our past to hold our future hostage?

There's no embarrassment in setback. The real question is whether we'll be man or woman enough to admit our mistake and learn from it without trying to smooth it over in order to save face. In the midst of our worst mistake or setback, God doesn't desert us. Sometimes, God allows Satan to put roadblocks in our path. Satan does it to tear us down, hoping we'll throw in the towel. But God uses those same roadblocks to test us and build us up. Whether or not we give in to Satan or turn to God will be the determining factor in our ongoing progress toward a life worth living or whether we choose the path of failure.

Management and leadership expert, Peter Drucker, has stated, "I would never promote to a top–level job a man who was not making mistakes .... otherwise he is sure to be mediocre." The more we come face to face with the setbacks of life, the easier it becomes to bounce back, to learn from our experience, and accept it for just what it is — a temporary speed bump in our path. Momentary setbacks mean little more than we just haven't succeeded — yet!

By the way, allow others the privilege of stumbling, too! Why should we have all the fun? If God gives us second chances and continues to encourage us, should we do anything less for others? Let them know it's okay to make a mistake once in a while, as long as they don't throw up their hands, fail to learn from it, and quit trying.

Water Walker

However as important as past experiences may be, let's not forget the importance of experiences yet to be. Some insist, "You can't teach an old dog new tricks". They may have been burned by past experience, causing them to shy away from attempting anything other than the tried–and–true. The normal adult tendency is to not stray too far from the familiar or launch out into new waters. We might fail. Or others will be watching and we might make a fool of ourselves. But circumstances change and we change. How sad that fear of the unknown might rob us of the courage to seize an opportunity that may never be available again.

For me, the Matthew 14 account of Peter walking on water with Jesus is one of the most thrilling in all Scripture. True, Peter is often chided for his lack of faith on this and other occasions. But, there's another side to the story.

Jesus has just miraculously fed a crowd of five thousand people (probably more than that when women and children were counted). John's account (John 6) of this same event tells us the people (and maybe the disciples were egging the crowd on, too) wanted to make Jesus king. But, in order to quell this enthusiasm, Jesus sends the disciples in a boat to the other side of the lake while he goes by himself to pray.

Boats are no big deal to these guys, especially Peter and Andrew who came from the fishing profession. The disciples have rowed a "considerable distance" (John's account indicates three–four miles) across the lake. It's late, during the "fourth watch" – three to six am. The disciples find themselves "buffeted" by the waves and genuinely fear for their lives.

Suddenly, Jesus shows up as he often does when and where we least expect him, walking on the water in the midst of the storm. The disciples certainly weren't looking for him. Assuming they were seeing a ghost, they didn't even recognize him. Only when Jesus

called out to them were they able to identify who was out there. "It's okay, guys. It's me."

Amid the awe, fear, confusion, and disbelief of the others, Peter has an intriguing reaction. "If it is you, Jesus, let me come walk with you on the water!" Not surprisingly, Jesus invites him to do just that. Meanwhile, we can picture the other disciples spurring Peter on. "Go for it, Peter!"

At that point, a whole series of questions probably flashed through Peter's mind. What have I done? Did Jesus really just invite me to walk on water? Has that brash side of me surfaced once again and I'm about to make a fool of myself? Do I really believe I can walk on water? No matter how this turns out, I'm going to be the topic of conversation around the campfire tonight!

But, contrary to the picture we often paint of Peter, I'm not so sure this was a totally impulsive move for him. It was more a calculated risk based on his trust of Jesus and the assurance that Jesus would have his back. Still, in the dark and on a tossing sea, Peter probably didn't step over the side of the boat with total confidence. I can picture him employing a plan B strategy, holding on to the side of the boat with one hand even as he steps in to the water. But he lets go and for the first time in all of recorded human history, an ordinary person walks on water!

But we know how the story ends. Peter takes a step or two – and begins to sink just like he and everybody else assumed he would. We always point to his lack of faith. But, unlike the other disciples, Peter got out of the boat! The real losers here were the eleven disciples still in the boat. I have to believe Jesus would have extended the same invitation to them. Instead, they opted for the role of comfortable spectator. "Let me watch, Jesus, but don't ask me to leave this boat!" They failed without ever leaving the boat! Reminds me of an observation from hockey great, Wayne Gretzke who pointed out, "You miss 100% of the shots you never take."

Someday I'm going to ...

Let's be honest, many of us are just like the disciples in the boat. We're eager to applaud others who tackle the unknown. But, when confronted with our own challenges, we allow our fear of what we don't know or the possibility that we may be a little less than perfect to keep us on the sidelines. In our heart, we know we have something to contribute. Jesus has called us to walk with him on the water, too. But, it's just easier to dream what could be or talk about what we're going to do than to actually take that first step. That's when we find ourselves muttering to ourselves, "Someday, I'm going to ...."

Can we even imagine the freedom and exhilaration Peter felt as he took his first tentative steps on the water? This would be a spiritual marker in Peter's life, an experience and a lesson he would never forget. I think it's worth noting that Peter was wise enough to know this was something he couldn't do in his own strength. Similarly, who knows what we might be able to accomplish if we boldly stepped into God's presence and pleasure instead of being so afraid we might fail? Just riding in the boat would never again be enough for Peter.

But, after a few steps, Peter did sink, didn't he? I have to believe this was a teachable moment for Peter, too. He didn't stay under water! Only Peter knew what it was like, when sinking under those waves, to have Jesus pull him up. That's got to make a lasting impression.

Like Peter, each time we get out of the boat, we discover fear is not necessarily fatal. Peter experienced a setback on this occasion. But, he's anything but a failure. Similarly, all of us experience setback from time to time. It's what we do with that experience that determines whether we fail or not.

At some point, Jesus calls every person to get out of the boat and go farther with him. Jesus loves us just as we are, but he loves us too much to have us simply remain in the boat. Whether or not we respond is our decision, but that decision will alter our life one

way or the other. If yes, we grow in faith and spiritual maturity. If not, we stagnate and become hardened.

I believe we sense that God has something more in mind for us than mere existence in the safe, the comfortable, the secure. We're made to grow. We're made to walk on water! When Satan would caution us to stay where we are, we're reminded that Jesus is on the water, not in the boat.

So what is on your "bucket list"? Will you allow your fear to govern your response to new opportunities and experiences? How can any Christian be content just to coast through life on past experience and past learning? After all, you can't learn to swim while standing on the beach.

I'm fascinated by airplanes and airports. Janie will tell you I've been known to drive miles out of my way just to watch planes take off and land. It staggers the imagination to realize something so huge can be on the ground in one city and in some city on the other side of the globe in a matter of a few hours.

But, as much as I enjoy watching planes from the ground, actually flying is one hundred times better. If we really want to soar in life, trusting God is the only way to fly. As one well–known airline advertises, he's ready when we are!

LIFE COACHING QUESTIONS

- *What experiences with God and others have had an indelible impression on who I am right now?*
- *How have my priorities changed or been reshaped by past experiences?*
- *Who in my life has been a significant influence and why? Who is that friend I can call at two a.m. and know they'll come? Who in my family loves me no matter what? A teacher who's made a difference?*

- *What mistakes have I made? What setbacks have I experienced and what have I learned from them? What are some of the lessons I've learned that I only wish I had learned earlier?*
- *What were my favorite school subjects? Why?*
- *What have I tried in the past for God and would like to try again, only doing it better this time?*
- *What have been some of the most satisfying times and experiences in my life to this point?*
- *What goals and milestones have I achieved to this point?*
- *What goals have gone unmet to this point? What regrets and "should'ves" continue to bug me?*
- *What new experiences are on my "bucket list"?*

FIND LASTING CONTENTMENT IN THE NICHE TAILOR-MADE FOR YOU

Snoopy sat droopy–eyed at the door to his doghouse. He lamented, "Yesterday I was a dog. Today I'm a dog. Tomorrow I'll probably still be a dog. There's so little hope for advancement."

More than we care to admit, all of us have a little Snoopy in us. Just in general, we like to think we deserve a better lot in life. In fact, in light of our life's circumstances, we often resort to a little game called "If Only …"

"IF ONLY …"
- I made more money
- Lived in that neighborhood or in that house
- Had that marriage
- Had those kids
- Drove that car
- Wore those clothes
- Had that job or career
- Did that for a living
- Had that educational degree

Understand, there's nothing particularly wrong with any of those desires. And, to be clear, no one would suggest we shouldn't attempt to improve our life situation. There's nothing virtuous about poverty. Nor is there anything wrong with ambition or wanting to better oneself. But as the be–all and end–all measure of our personal contentment, any of these circumstances are pretty shallow and will likely leave us still searching. When we focus on what we don't have, discontentment can't be far behind.

Real life's contentment has little to do with circumstances or possessions anyway. Much discontentment is, at its root, the result of comparing ourselves and our circumstances with others and trying to be someone we were never meant to be. As Trappist monk Thomas Merton noted, "A tree brings glory to God by being a tree." In the same way, you and I bring glory to God by being the person he created us to be.

The words of Paul call us beyond our circumstances to something better and more satisfying. "I've learned by now to be quite content whatever my circumstances. I'm just as happy with little as with much, with much as with little. I've found the recipe for being happy whether full or hungry, hands full or hands empty. Whatever I have, wherever I am, I can make it through anything in the One who makes me who I am" (Philippians 4:11–13 MSG). Genuine, lasting contentment is possible only when we discover God's life design for *us* (our NICHE) and refuse to be conformed to the world's mold or the agenda of others, whether they be parents, friends, or associates.

When we realize how special we are to God and that he created us to find lasting contentment in his NICHE for us, then only three questions really need to be considered:

- Am I becoming the person God created me to be?
- Am I seeking God and his will more than anything else?
- Am I in the center of his will to the best of my understanding?

Bottom line, the one key to personal contentment and fulfillment can be simply stated. *There's no need for us to be like anyone or better than anyone as long as we're the best "us" we can be.* It's my firm belief that I am more likely to become the best "me" I can be when God's NICHE for me guides my life's path. The clear teaching of Scripture would seem to agree. "Let's just go ahead and be what we were made to be, without enviously or pridefully comparing ourselves with each other, or trying to be something we aren't." (Romans 12:6,MSG)

Then, guided and directed by our one overarching priority — our relationship with Jesus Christ — the rest of life is viewed as "roles" for godly influence and service to others.

- Does the way I relate to my spouse honor God and lift up his name?
- How about the way I relate to my children?
- Those persons I work closely with? Do they see Christ at all in the things I say and do?
- Does the way I use my time and my financial resources reflect that core priority?
- What does my decision–making in key relationships say about my desire to honor God?
- On a more personal level (that's a key relationship, too!), do my personal habits — what I watch on TV, what I listen to, what I read, what I eat and drink, how I care for my physical body, etc. — in any way, bring embarrassment to him?
- More to the point, do I ever feel the need to "check" my priority loyalty to God at the door when I enter certain places, meet with certain people, or engage in certain activities?

When all of life is viewed as a means of honoring God, we possess a philosophy of life we can take with us to the office on Monday, to the golf course, or to the mall. God is God seven days

a week. As motivational speaker Zig Ziglar put it, we don't serve a part–time God!

Writing Your Personal Purpose Statement

Author and leadership consultant John Maxwell has stated that your life's purpose, the very reason for your existence, can be summed up in one sentence! Now, I don't know that all of us can articulate our purpose just that succinctly. But, let me say up front, the length of our life's purpose statement is not the issue, anyway. The point is that we spend time crafting that statement and pursuing it in real life.

The neat thing is we get to determine, with God, what that purpose will be. Of course, honoring God and being a growing disciple are both givens for any Christian. But, a personal purpose statement strives to be more specific than that. Based on what you've discovered, to this point, about your NICHE, let me challenge you to begin creating your own purpose statement.

- *GOD CREATED ME TO _____*
- *HOW WOULD GOD HAVE ME SPEND MY LIFE?*
- *WHAT MARK WOULD I LIKE TO LEAVE ON MY WORLD?*

If you need to use more than one sentence, that's okay. Just spend time with God as you begin developing your statement.

I emphasize the word "begin" because this is something you work on over time. Start where you are now in crafting your statement and keep tweaking it as you discover more about this person God created you to be. From time to time, as you revisit your responses to the NICHE acrostic, you may gain new insights about your purpose. You may need to adjust your purpose statement as you acquire new

abilities, interests, experiences, relationships, and enter new seasons of life. Like much of life, you're a work in progress, too.

In fact, I would encourage going one step further. Using your purpose statement as a starting point, develop accompanying goals for the next six months to one year. Write them down! Dr. Gail Matthews, psychology professor at Dominican University in California, cites research based on a study with 267 people. She found that those who simply write down their goals are 42% more likely to reach them. It's truer than we can imagine: Blessed are those who aim at nothing for verily they shall hit it!

If done well, this becomes much more than just a paper exercise to gather dust as you move on with your life. Here are some ways your purpose statement and accompanying goals can prove invaluable for you:

1. Forces me to think more deeply about who I am and my life's purpose than I ever have before.

2. Guides investment of time and energy. Author Henry Blackaby says the one key to time stewardship is staying on God's agenda. That's why I believe the greatest time and energy stewardship tool available to us is our personal purpose statement. That one item will articulate what we understand to be God's agenda for us and a road map for our future.

3. When we're often confronted with choosing between the merely good and the best God has to offer in terms of relationships, how we will spend our time and energy, the use of material resources available to us, and so on, our purpose statement can guide our selections. Our purpose statement becomes the basis for determining priorities and saying yes or no to new opportunities.

   For many of us, learning to say "no" is difficult. Yet that one small word may be one of the holiest words in all of the English language. Not that we want to simply be contrary,

but the ability to say no for the right reasons, without guilt or second-guessing, can be awfully liberating.

4. You operate out of your strengths more often than your limitations.

5. Results in a greater sense of direction and motivation.

6. Your purpose statement allows you to focus on pleasing God, not others. And, let's face it, after 60+ years of life experiences, I've come to realize that pleasing God is often easier than pleasing others!

7. Your purpose statement will give you hope when discouragement, emotions, and circumstances are letting you down.

Remember that advice I received from a counselor friend. *Under God*, decide who you are and how your life will be spent. Don't let others make that decision for you. We live in a culture where some abdicate their choices and options to media, celebrities, and any other voice that screams the loudest. After all, we reason, they wouldn't be where they are if they didn't know what they were talking about. But, when we become who others say we should be, we often find we don't particularly care for who we've become.

I'm not suggesting every message we hear from others should be ignored. There may well be wisdom in their advice. But, as we become better acquainted with our NICHE, hopefully we will have a filter for evaluating those messages.

We said it earlier, but it bears repeating. Despite what well-intentioned persons in our life would suggest, we cannot be anyone we want to be. However, we are perfectly capable of being the person God created us to be. That open-door potential is there. It's our choice whether we walk through the door or not. We CAN be everything God uniquely created us to be.

Jon Gordon sums it up well. "You are here for a reason and the most important thing you can do in life is to find, live and share

your purpose. It's the one thing in life that truly matters and if you don't pursue it everything else is meaningless."

A Verse for Life

In Acts 13:36, there is an easily–overlooked verse of Scripture that deserves more than passing note. There we read, "Now when David had served God's purpose in his own generation, he fell asleep; he was buried with his ancestors and his body decayed."

You and I were created for *this* moment, for our generation, for a life worth living. As created beings, you and I have no right and certainly aren't entitled to simply exist for our own pleasure and comfort. God created us for and is calling us to a life of significance and meaning, one that will make a difference in our own day and in our own life.

Don't misunderstand. Awareness of our NICHE and living out of our sweet spot is not always smooth sailing. It requires intentionality and discipline. Sometimes it entails just plain old hard work. But, given the alternative of simply drifting through life with no sense of direction and uncertain of the outcome, could we possibly imagine a life more meaningful and satisfying than one in which we complete God's purpose for us and then simply die? No regrets. What a way to go. Talk about going out on a high note!

SKILLS & INTERESTS CATEGORIES

Athletics

Art

Drama

Music

Writing

Public speaking

Mechanical and auto repairs

Carpentry

Coaching

Tutoring

Cooking and entertaining

Financial planning

Foreign languages

Gardening

Home repair

Organizing events and programs

Reading

Research

Sewing

Storytelling

Science

Mathematics and problem solving
Mechanical abilities
Woodworking
Outdoors skills
Inventing
Computers
Photography
Teaching
Helping others
Leadership

SPIRITUAL GIFTS PRAYER GUIDE

This prayer guide is designed to help you *pray through with God* your interests, abilities, and spiritual gifts. By doing so, you gain insight into how God is leading you to ministry and service for Him. There are no right or wrong answers. Your response should reflect you, your thoughts, and how God has uniquely created you.

=================================

1. How would <u>you</u> describe your personality? (Choose one from each pair)

    a. a leader   a follower
    b. outgoing   reserved
    c. enjoy working with others   prefer to work alone
    d. enjoy being out front   prefer behind the scenes
    e. task–oriented   people–oriented
    f. organized   spontaneous
    g. optimistic   pessimistic

2. The qualities and character traits I would like most to be a part of my life are

    _____

3. What roles of leadership and/or service have I attempted that were fulfilling for me?

    _____

4. What roles of leadership and/or service have I attempted and received affirmation or encouragement from others?

    _____

5. With proper training for a particular area of service, I can see myself

    _____

6. If I could really make a difference for Christ and His Church in my world, I'd like to

    _____

7. The area(s) of ministry and service *in my church or my community* that I feel the greatest interest and enthusiasm about are

    _____

8. If I could design or choose an area of service in which I would feel most comfortable, most fulfilled, and most used of God, it would be

_____

9. Based on my background, experience, training, interests, and understanding of God's will for my life, I believe God has given me these spiritual gifts:

1. _____ 2. _____ 3. _____

Printed in the United States
By Bookmasters

CPSIA information can be obtained
at www.ICGtesting.com
Printed in the USA
JSHW030304260722
28426JS00002B/4

COMPARE AND CONTRAST

Compare moray eels and oarfish. In what ways are they different?

(15 meters) long! A long, red fin runs along the oarfish's back and rises to a high crest on top of the head.

The rabbitfish, a small relative of sharks, has a head and teeth resembling a rabbit. Frogfish have bumpy bodies that blend into their surroundings of sponges and coral reefs. They use their fins to walk underwater. Some deep-water fish such as anglerfish and hatchetfish have adapted to their dark environment with body parts that glow!

A leafy sea dragon like this can be found in South Australia.

SHARKS!

Sharks are fish that have a skeleton made of cartilage instead of bone. Cartilage lets sharks bend and twist. It is lighter than bone, so this helps sharks swim fast. There are more than 400 species of sharks. Most sharks are smart and have well-developed senses. Many sharks can see well even in murky water, and some

dwarf lantern shark
(*Etmopterus perryi*)

Dwarf lantern sharks live in almost total darkness. Light from their bellies attracts prey.

sharks can detect prey using only their sense of smell. Most people are afraid of sharks, but only a few species are known to attack humans. Some sharks—including lemon, mako, and thrasher sharks—are considered valuable as food.

Sharks are among the oldest living things. They live in all the oceans of the world, even in the cold Arctic waters and the seas around Antarctica. The largest is the whale shark, which can grow up to 59 feet (18 meters) long and weigh 20 tons (18 metric tons). The smallest shark is the dwarf lantern shark, which is only about 7.5 inches (19 centimeters) long.

Hammerhead sharks rarely bother people. Their favorite food is the stingray.

WHAT DO FISH EAT?

Almost all fish eat other fish that are smaller than themselves. The smallest fish eat tiny water plants and animals called plankton. Freshwater fish may eat algae, plants, insects, frogs, and other fishes' larvae and eggs.

Sharks are at the top of the food chain in the ocean. Besides fish, some sharks eat seals, dolphins, squid, and

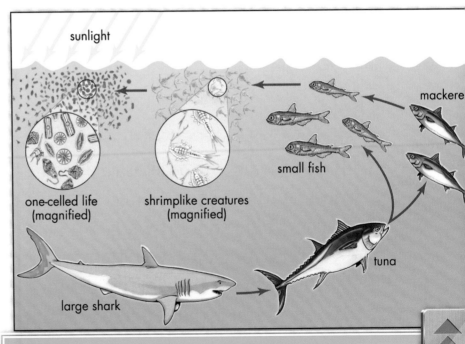

sunlight

one-celled life (magnified)

shrimplike creatures (magnified)

small fish

mackere

tuna

large shark

Almost everything in the ocean is part of a food chain.

Like sharks, stingrays have cartilage instead of bones. This helps them be more flexible.

even sea turtles. Smaller fish feed on mollusks (including octopuses, shrimp, clams, and squid), sea stars, and other organisms that live in shallow water or in deeper water. Fish that live in the deepest part of the ocean cannot be picky. There is no light or plant life there. These fish feed on other deep-sea animals or on whatever scraps drift down to them.

THINK ABOUT IT
Different kinds of fish eat many different things. Why do you think this is?

THE LIFE CYCLE OF FISH

All fish hatch from eggs. Usually, females release eggs into the water and males fertilize them by releasing sperm. After a time, larvae hatch from the eggs. Soon, the larva forms a skeleton and develops fins and scales. Many eggs and larvae are eaten by other fish. Some kinds of fish try to protect

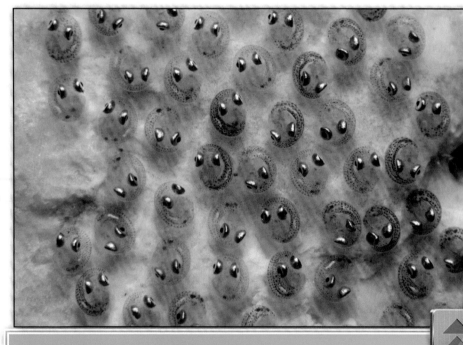

Most fish eggs are transparent, or see-through. A yolk sac provides food for the larvae after they hatch.

A female guppy may give birth to 60 or more live young at a time.

their eggs by hiding them, but most fish do not protect their eggs or their young. To increase the chance that some young will survive, a female releases hundreds, thousands, or even millions of eggs at a time. Sometimes the eggs are fertilized in the female's body and hatch there. The young are then born live from the female. Guppies, some sharks, and surfperches give birth to live young. After a fish grows into an adult, it will be ready to spawn.

VOCABULARY

Spawn means to produce young, especially in large numbers. Fish spawn by releasing eggs and sperm.

WHY WE NEED FISH

Fish are food for many animals. Bears, seals, and many birds consume fish as part of their diet. Fish are also an important source of food for humans. People all over the world eat many different kinds of fish, including cod, herring, and tuna.

Many bears eat fish as part of their diet.

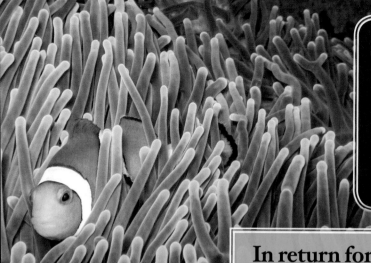

COMPARE AND CONTRAST

Compare and contrast the ways that fish are important to people and to the environment.

In return for a safe home, clownfish help clean sea anemones.

Fish are also an important part of many ecosystems. Goby fish eat seaweeds that would kill coral reefs. Fish help control diseases such as malaria, yellow fever, and the zika virus by eating mosquito larvae. And through their waste products, fish provide nutrients that help plants grow. All of these things help keep ecosystems in balance. Additionally, researchers use some fish in medical studies that may one day treat or cure heart disease, skin cancer, and muscular dystrophy.

PET FISH

Ichthyologists are not the only people who like to watch fish. Fish are one of the most popular pets that people keep in their homes. Goldfish, guppies, and bettas are easy to care for and fun to watch. Koi, a type of carp, come in many beautiful colors and are often kept in ponds in backyards or in parks. Many people set up an aquarium, a special glass tank, which can hold several types of fish. Home aquariums may hold as little as 1 gallon (3.8 liters) of water

◀◀ Koi may be a solid color or have up to three different colors.

or more than 100 gallons (3,785 l)!

Large public aquariums help people learn about fish and their habitats. Most aquariums have many different kinds of fish from different parts of the world. Some have underwater tunnels that let people see fish swim around and above them. Many aquariums have tide pool exhibits or small tanks that allow visitors to touch some types of fish.

Some aquariums are large enough to hold a whale shark, along with many smaller species of fish.

MAJOR THREATS TO FISH

Human activity can cause major damage to fish populations. When people build dams on rivers the flow of water in the rivers is lowered. That may prevent fish from swimming upstream to spawn. Wetlands are filled in to make way for buildings. Sometimes people release fish into areas where that type of fish has never lived before. If the fish have no natural enemies in their new habitat, they can quickly multiply and may wipe out fish that were already living there.

Oil spills kill fish and other sea life.

People dump garbage and sewage into creeks, rivers, ponds, lakes, and oceans. Factories or cities sometimes release harmful chemicals, oil, and other wastes into water. These can poison the fish that live in the water. Global warming is increasing the temperature of Earth's water. The warmer water kills some plants and other organisms that fish eat. Another problem is overfishing. When too many fish of the same species are caught, the species may become extinct.

THINK ABOUT IT
What threats to fish are caused by people? Are there threats that are caused by nature?

Plastic bags, fishing line, and other types of litter kill fish and their food supplies.

How We Can Help Fish

We can help fish by not building new dams and by removing dams that are no longer needed. In some areas, fish ladders have been built to help fish move past dams so they can spawn. Protecting wetlands is another way to help protect fish. Many places are working to prevent people from accidentally introducing fish into areas where the fish do not belong.

Fish ladders help salmon and steelhead make it past dams to reach their spawning grounds.

Some fish farms raise endangered fish to release into the wild, instead of as food.

Fish farming helps prevent overfishing of some species. Some types of fish, such as trout, can be easily bred in captivity. Once hatched, they are raised in tanks or ponds. The grown fish are then sold for food.

Preventing oil spills and other forms of pollution will help keep ocean fish healthy. Some countries are working to stop global warming. This will help keep our rivers and oceans from becoming too warm for fish.

The Wonderful World of Fish

Fish may be the oldest vertebrates in the world, but we still have a lot to learn about them. New species of fish are discovered every year. Some fish, like the tiny mandarin dragonet, are beautiful. Others, such as piranhas and anglerfish, are scary-looking. Fish live in streams, in rivers, and even in pools in dark underground caves. They live in sunny

COMPARE AND CONTRAST

Compare and contrast the ways fish are like people.

waters and in the deepest part of the ocean where light never reaches.

Some fish live in groups, called schools, to protect themselves from predators. Other fish, like the moray eel, prefer to be alone. No matter what they look like, or where they live, fish are an important part of Earth, and they need our protection.

Mandarin dragonets are some of the most colorful fish in the ocean.

GLOSSARY

aquarium A glass tank in which living water animals or plants are kept.

cold-blooded Having a body temperature that is not regulated by the body.

ecosystem A community of living things interacting with their environment.

fertilize To join the necessary reproductive parts (e.g. a sperm unites with an egg) in order to create life; to increase the likelihood of reproduction or growth.

global warming A warming of Earth's atmosphere and oceans.

larva A young form of an animal that looks very different from its parents.

malaria A fever that is passed on to humans by the bite of mosquitoes.

migrate To move from one place or region to another.

muscular dystrophy An inherited disease that causes increasing weakness of muscles.

plankton Small plants and animals that float or drift in a body of water.

predator An animal that lives by killing and eating other animals.

reproduce To succesfully make new organisms through fertilization, development, and giving birth.

sea anemone A boneless sea animal that looks like a flower and has brightly colored tentacles.

species A group of organisms that have common features and can reproduce young of the same kind.

tropical Having to do with an area that is very warm and wet or humid.

wetlands Lands or areas, such as marshes and swamps, that have much moisture in the soil.